The Man Who Wanted
to Meet God

The Man Who Wanted to Meet God

Myths and Stories that Explain the Inexplicable

His Holiness Shantanand Saraswati

Bell Tower
New York

Published by Bell Tower, an imprint of Harmony Books, a division of
Crown Publishers, Inc., 201 East 50th Street, New York, New York
10022. Member of the Crown Publishing Group.
A few of the stories in this book originally appeared in *Good Company*,
published by the Society for the Study of Normal Psychology in 1987
and by Element Books in 1992.
Random House, Inc. New York, Toronto, London, Sydney, Auckland.

Bell Tower and colophon are trademarks of Crown Publishers, Inc.

Manufactured in the United States of America

Design by Linda Kocur

Library of Congress Cataloging-in-Publication Data is available upon
request.

ISBN 0-517-88520-4

10 9 8 7 6 5 4 3 2 1

First Edition

Contents

Introduction

Can a story change our lives? Perhaps. Can it change our response to the needs and challenges of the present moment? Certainly. Then would the repeated use of stories and the recalling of incidents and the feelings they arouse transform and change our lives by changing our responses? It is one of the chief messages of this book that this does indeed happen, especially when the stories are told with a specific purpose: helping people to discover their true selves.

The stories and myths gathered in this book come from a series of audiences granted by one of the great spiritual teachers of this century, His Holiness Shantanand Saraswati, the elder Shankaracharya of Jyotir Math in Northern India. He is the head of an ancient tradition of knowledge and meditation. One of the ways in which His Holiness Shantanand Saraswati has taught this knowledge is by using stories and myths from the past as well as incidents from his own experience and from contemporary life. Even when some of these stories and myths may be familiar from other sources such as the *Mahabharata* and

the *Ramayana,* the way in which they are told in his words and
with his interpretation casts fresh light on the narratives and
makes them shine with new meanings. He uses stories to answer questions and make them practical for everyday living.
The depth of his spiritual understanding and his feeling for
humanity as a whole are revealed in the most intimate and
approachable ways in these stories. As we read them again and
again we will find their themes and images and sense of fun returning in our memories to succour us in moments of difficulty
and enliven times of dullness.

The meditation referred to in the commentaries on the
stories consists of repeating a sacred word or mantra. The knowledge associated with the meditation is the Advaita, or nondual-
ist philosophy, which in its essence goes back at least as far as
the Vedic period (1500 BC) and which was given its fullest state-
ment by the great philosopher and teacher Shankara, who lived
more than one thousand years ago. Shankara founded four seats
in different parts of India to continue his teaching, and the
succession in the northern seat of Jyotir Math is in direct line
from this great teacher and philosopher.

For some thirty years His Holiness has given instruction on
meditation and the Advaita philosophy to members of a society
in London, the Society for the Study of Normal Psychology,
which is devoted to investigating the nature of consciousness
and to making practical use of these investigations in daily life.
The founder of this society, the late Dr. Francis Roles, and others associated with the society, made many journeys to India to
put questions to His Holiness Shantanand Saraswati and this
material has been taken from the record of their conversations.

In most religious traditions the use of myths, parables, or
fables plays an important part in teaching and in making pre-

cepts memorable. His Holiness Shantanand Saraswati has recently made a significant contribution to explaining why this should be so. The revival of an interest in myth in the West prompted questions on this subject to him. He was asked, first, whether universal myths were stored and released by universal memory, and second, how these myths related to creative imagination in the human soul.

His view is startling both for its simplicity and its originality. He states that the purpose of myths is to explain the inexplicable and that they centre upon the oneness of God. They attract because they give delight as well as instruction and they act like winds sweeping away the clouds of ignorance.

The whole passage repays much study for its thought-provoking and challenging statements:

> Myths are common to all civilisations. In the dawn of different cultures and civilisations the human spirit, wishing to pass on its knowledge to future generations, has used allegorical narratives to pass on its experiences and insights. Myths are a combination of creative imagination and reason. There is an element of creative imagination involved in an artistic narrative even when based on a factual foundation. Myths are not figments of imagination. For instance, God exists but is not empirically perceptible. There is some intuition of a power which cannot be indicated by pointing a finger to it, so inspired beings in all cultures try to build up a mythical structure so that those who have no such direct intuition can grasp the idea and then make themselves open to that experience. This is how myths arise, not to deceive but to explain the inexplicable.

Myths give pleasure because their central theme is always human experience. They are a whole and therefore connected and correlated; one word can recall the whole story. Analytical explanations not based on human experience remain unconnected and are, therefore, difficult to hold in memory. That is why ordinary people are not attracted to them. Empiricists try to explain everything empirically, but having found the limitations of this method they turn to find traces of deeper knowledge in myth.

There are four ways by which knowledge is received. The first is from experience, the second through reason which lies just beyond experience. The third is through the Word, the Vedas, or traditional scriptures, which give knowledge that cannot otherwise be known. The fourth is through the utterings of great men, wise men, holy men, who sometimes create mythical stories to convey the essence of their own experience allegorically—these are the myths. To ignore them as meaningless is to deprive oneself of something real and artistic. Wise men have no axe to grind, but they can be creative and artistic in presenting what they have experienced or realized.

Some fantastic myths are the invention of men who are not so wise! They let loose their fancy and concoct a story simply to impress or deceive. These one must ignore.

Myths are messages of a metaphysical kind. They are allegorical and artistic expressions. To try to look for history in them is a fruitless exercise. Each culture creates its own myths. They are similar because they are all human. There is no particular body of myth deposited anywhere, but conditions giving rise to similar myths do abound in different places. Consciousness is creative and creativity is not copying. Similarities are either accidental or borrowed. Myth helps to clear away the sheath of ignorance. For example, the sun is always shining and those who are not blind can always see the sun. If clouds come over then the sun may be hidden. When the wind blows the clouds away then one can see the sun again. Likewise these myths are like winds which clear away the clouds of ignorance so that the truth can be seen again clearly. Realization is already there. The Self, therefore, needs no realization but the clouds of ignorance must go.

These myths and questions are not new. The questions and answers are all raised again and again in time. They appear new to each person, but only because of the cloud in his experience. Myths have a message. The qualities associated with God are love, mercy, justice, charity, truth, bliss, rescue of the meek, punishment of evil, and protection of the weak. These are there for us to learn and translate into action.

The essence of all myths centres on the oneness of God. Some prefer the abstract concept, others prefer a concrete form and depict God in the drama of creation—this is the realistic approach. They call God by various names and describe Him according to their culture. The wise look for unity, and poets give descriptive glory. Ordinary man enjoys whatever he receives through his family tradition. Very few seek the truth of His unity, conscious freedom, and blissful detachment. The Absolute must be one—it cannot be two. If there were two Absolutes then there could never be one truth, and duality would always prevail. There would be no peace, no reason, no freedom, and no permanent bliss. Every vision or myth would be incomplete, blurred, and ambiguous. Uncertainty would reign everywhere.

[Earlier His Holiness said] Whenever an illustration is presented in story form it sheds light on only one aspect of the Absolute and we must always keep in mind that the stories only lead to what cannot be put into words. They never include everything that the Absolute is or could be and are never complete as the Absolute is.

It is sometimes said that we need new myths to live by today. The great myths of the past are the creations of great and wise men. They are the expression in allegorical form of profound spiritual experience. Here again is a thought worth contemplating: that great art and great literature derive from the greatness of soul of their originators.

"Consciousness," His Holiness said, "is creative." When some years ago he was asked a question about whether new forms were needed for art and literature, he answered that there was nothing wrong with the arts and their rules. The fault lies in the lack of real experience in the makers of art. Present-day society, influenced by the shallowness of much art today, has lost touch with appreciation. The answer lies in this: "When a man of good being takes to experience and expression, then art manifests and it goes straight to the heart of people. Rules are not what matter most; it is being and experience that matter. Make *men* and they will make *art*."

The teaching or philosophy of Advaita, nondualism, can be helpful to anyone wishing to lead a united and universal life. His Holiness Shantanand Saraswati says this knowledge is "not for any single race, colour, creed, or nation, but for everybody, anywhere, any time, who is looking for it."

NOTE: Over the years the Shankaracharya used many of the same stories to illustrate various aspects of nondualism. Different versions of some of these stories appeared in an earlier publication, *Good Company* (Element Books, 1992).

Wherever possible English translations of Sanskrit words have been given. *Atman* and *Param Atman* have been translated as Self and Universal Self, and *Brahman* as the Absolute. In Indian myth there is much reference to the holy man, sometimes as a mahatma, and sometimes as a saint; the inner, or spiritual, meaning of the holy man is that of the Universal Self.

Attachment

Thousands of devotees take a dip in the holy waters of the Ganges and gain by it. A trader is happy when there is a profit. But what about a loss?

In this 'trade' of life, all of us want to make a profit and avoid a loss. The first two verses of the *Isha Upanishad* tell us the way. They say:

> The entire living and non-living world constituting this universe should be taken as a manifestation of one single Absolute. Make your living in this world with the things provided for you, without desiring money from anyone else. The Absolute does not assert His ownership over what He gives to the world, like air, water, and food. Similarly, while using them for your living, you should not consider them as belonging to you, and yourself as the owner.
>
> Desire a life of a hundred years thus lived full of action. There is no other way to avoid a coating of evil while leading a human life.

According to the *Bhagavad-Gita,* Arjuna refused to fight the war of the *Mahabharata,* and Krishna had to persuade him to do so. He explained to Arjuna that even if he did not heed his advice, Arjuna's own nature and temperament would force him into battle. In this way our nature, habits, and tendencies drive us into good and bad actions. Therefore we should try to change the evil tendencies in our nature for better ones.

People often complain that although they have been practising *Bhakti* (the path of devotion) or meditation for a number of years, yet they do not appear to be deriving any benefit from it. This is because their tendencies and nature have not changed.

We should bear in mind that whatever the Creator has given to the world, He has given it up to the world. He no longer claims any ownership of it. We should also cultivate the habit of using and enjoying it as his gift and not as our own property. This attitude will correct our evil tendencies, and then the practice of devotion or meditation will begin bearing fruit.

It is not gold or worldly possessions which are evil, only identification with them.

Once four businessmen set out on a trip carrying firearms for protection. They met a mahatma on the way, who warned them not to go that way as it was dangerous. They did not listen to him and said that they were well-equipped to face any danger. As they went farther, they found a bar of gold lying on the ground. Rejoicing at their find, they wrapped it up in a piece of cloth with the idea of dividing it among themselves.

As night fell, two of them went to a neighbouring village to buy some food, while two stayed behind. When they had gone, those who stayed behind felt tempted to keep the bar for themselves and conspired to shoot the other two when they returned with the food.

The two who had gone to the village had a hearty meal in a café; while returning with the food for the other two, they also succumbed to the temptation of keeping the bar for themselves and plotted to do away with their friends. Therefore they mixed poison with the food they were taking back to them.

When they returned with the food, the other two shot them dead. They were hungry, so they at once devoured the food brought for them. They fell asleep, never to wake again!

Next morning the same mahatma passed by on his way to the river for his daily bath. He found the four lying dead, and the bar of gold wrapped in a cloth. He threw the gold into the river so that it might not do further mischief.

This is how mishaps occur in daily life owing to our reasoning being poisoned by evil tendencies. If we regard and use everything as a gift from the Absolute, and thus practise devotion, then our reasoning becomes clear and we can lead a long and happy life as expressed in the Upanishad verses.

Evil associations cause evil tendencies in our reasoning, and they, in turn, result in evil actions. Good associations cause good tendencies, and result in good actions. We should all try to achieve a long life full of happiness and useful action by following this teaching of the Upanishad. Such a life would be good for us and good for the world.

THE MONKEY ON THE ROOF OF THE TRAIN

A monkey sat on the roof of a railway carriage, and when a passenger put his head out of the window, the monkey quietly descended, stole his cap and climbed back onto the roof. The bystanders advised the passenger to give the monkey something to eat, in order to get his cap back. When he passed up a banana, the monkey held the banana in one hand but hung on to the cap with the other. When offered a second banana, the monkey took it but dropped the cap onto the railway line where it was irretrievably lost!

We are all temperamentally greedy like the monkey, and there are innumerable temptations in the world to attract our greed. The force of these attractions is irresistible, and we continue to fall victim to them all the time. These forces are desire, sex, anger, attachment, greed, vanity, and jealousy, which keep on beguiling us so that we find it difficult to escape. The only way out is renunciation. It looks difficult, but it comes with practice. Just practise transferring your love of these attractions to the Absolute.

Attachment to worldly things is the root cause of all our trouble, for we little realize that it is all false, and that we are bound to be deceived if we take worldly things seriously. Once your mind is focused on love for the Absolute, the world will cease to tempt you.

THE FATHER AND SON AT THE STATION

A young man left for Bombay from a village in the state of Uttar Pradesh. His wife was pregnant, and she gave birth to a son four months after he had gone. This young man had to stay in Bombay for twelve years; he could not afford to come home, but continued to correspond. In the course of time the boy grew up and used to read the letters and write to his father.

One day, all of a sudden, the young boy wanted to go and see his father, so he left for the long journey to the station. At the same time, the father, now an older man, wanted to come home and started from Bombay and reached this same station. The father had to stay the night at the station because the village was too far away, so they were both there on the same evening. The father booked a waiting room in which to spend the night. The young boy did not have any money, so he had to sleep outside; he had a cold, was coughing quite a lot, and had a slight temperature. The man found that he could not sleep because of the constant coughing so he called the station-master to remove the boy from the vicinity of the waiting room. The boy was removed and suffered a great deal. In the morning as he was about to leave for the village, the man looked at this boy and, finding something familiar in his facial characteristics, enquired who he was. The boy gave all his particulars, his name, his village and his father's name. The man asked why he was there, and the boy said he was going to Bombay to see his father. The man realized that this was his son and embraced him and wept for the sin he had committed the previous night—to have removed his own son because the boy's cough was disturbing his sleep.

If you are pure within then all your promptings, whatever message you get from within, will stand up for everyone in the world, not just your own son. Because the Self is the same every-where, purity sees the Self, not the son. If one has cleansed one-self, then certainly one's promptings will be universal not individual. Whatever one is doing, one has to see if one is doing it for everyone, for oneself, or for one's relatives, for the things one cherishes, or the organisation or nation to which one be-longs. That is the thing to watch.

The Holy Man and the Beautiful Woman

Where does the feeling of wonder at creation come from? It seems so strange that one does not feel this more. One would have expected it to be the main feeling of people on earth—amazement at being here at all! Is it connected with the memory of something different?

The feeling of wonder is a pure feeling because with it the question immediately arises in the beholder: "What is the cause of the creation of such beautiful scenes?" He immediately enters into the realm of the causal world, thus reaching the ultimate source, not only of what has been created, but the source of creation itself.

With this feeling, the beauty that is let loose in creation is allowed to grow and become all the more enhanced. But if you do not have this sense of wonder at the beauty of creation, then immediately some attachment prevails. A desire for greater involvement arises and you want to possess those examples of beauty. Once you have possessed them, you want to use them. This it seems is one way of becoming attached to the outer forms of beauty. Then in fact all you succeed in doing is to pollute the beauty!

If, on the contrary, you have seen something which is repulsive, then you want to destroy it. So in both cases whether you like or dislike something, if you are without the sense of wonder, you are going to be the means of corruption as far as the beauty of the whole is concerned. But if you keep the sense of wonder in viewing creation, whether it is likeable or hateful, beautiful or ugly, then in neither case is any corruption added to the situation. In the first case you will work for its enhancement; in the second case, you will not do anything harmful to add to the misery.

Take the example of the *sannyasin* (a holy man who has renounced the world) who happened to see a very beautiful woman in the street. He continued to gaze at her, so some of the householders who came along said to him: "You are a *sannyasin* and you have given up the world. Is it good for you to look at the beauty of a woman for it will certainly lead you towards the sensual world!" The sannyasin replied, "My dear friends, I am looking at the Creator who is just making play in His creation through this beautiful form. I am not merely looking at the physical body, I am enjoying everything which is the cause of the manifest form."

So one should cultivate this feeling of wonder at creation in whatever form it may present itself. Enjoy the beauty and by doing so you will enhance it.

2

Birth and Death

KING JANAKA'S DREAMS

There are only three ways of establishing the validity of the subtle and causal worlds. The first is the scriptures, the Vedic knowledge which is said to be the result of divine utterances. If the scriptures say it then we believe in it. Secondly, we gather the knowledge ourselves and through inference establish the difference between the physical, subtle, and causal bodies, and the Self which pervades everything. Thirdly, in certain cases individuals acquire insight. Only they can transcend the limits of these physical boundaries and see the realm of the subtle world. It is usually in these three ways that some knowledge about this subject is made available to individuals in this world.

From all this it is possible to come to the realization that the physical body is a limited world which has no validity of itself and no means of establishing relationship directly with the causal or spiritual world except through inferences derived from knowledge.

Take the example of King Janaka.

Once, when on his travels, he broke his journey and went to sleep. In his sleep he had a dream in which he was entering a village. At the moment when he was going through the door of a house in this village, a dog came up behind him and bit him. Blood flowed from the dog-bite, and King Janaka was in great pain; many people gathered round him, and a doctor was called. The doctor put some ointment on the wound, but because it was astringent it increased the pain in the leg. The king cried out with pain, and this awoke him from the dream.

When he woke up he found neither the village, the people, the dog, nor the painful leg! How did all this happen? Where did the dog come from? Who got the doctor? Who assembled the people and created the village? The only conclusion is that the subtle body creates a world of its own and enacts all those things. The cause of such a dream drama arises out of the cherished desires which are in one's causal body. These unfulfilled desires somehow create a dream world which seems to find expression for them. So the whole experience of the dream is a proof of the existence of the subtle and causal worlds.

The same applies in this life and to birth and death. When the physical body is about to die, all these experiences are retained in the subtle and causal bodies. The Self, of course, is neither born nor dies.

If this question of birth and death is taken in the light of the three levels of existence, we can see there is no difficulty in understanding it, just as in our common life there is unconsciousness occasionally, sleeping, dreaming, waking, and *samadhi* (enlightened state). All these states can be experienced right here in this body. So in the same way, in the greater plan, birth and death are just a change of level; the initial connection is always kept through the Self, but most of the experiences are left behind, just as we leave the experience of our dream, yet something is carried on.

On another occasion King Janaka dreamt that he was attacked and lost his throne, and then wandered round penniless and persecuted by everyone. He eventually entered the forest, starving. He managed to gather enough fruit and vegetables to make a meal, but just when he had prepared it, two bulls appeared and trampled it all. At this the king began to weep and woke up to find real tears wetting his shoulder. He then called all the pundits and asked them to answer the question, "Which was real—the dream which produced the tears, or his seat on the throne?" He said he would handsomely reward anyone who could answer, but would severely punish anyone who answered if the answer proved false. Various people tried to answer, but the answers were incomplete and those who offered them were duly punished.

There was a cripple called Ashtavakra (which means 'bent in eight places'). While he was in the womb his father used to chant Vedic verses, and when he made mistakes the foetus shouted from the womb correcting him. The father said, "You are still in the womb, don't show me any respect, and dare to correct me—what will you be like when you are born?" So he put a curse on the baby, who was born crippled and bent in eight places. This man came to answer the question and started to climb the steps to the throne. Because of his handicap he fell halfway up and the courtiers all laughed at him. He also started to laugh, which greatly surprised them, so they asked, "Why do you laugh?" He then said, "You laughed first so tell me why you laughed." They replied that they laughed because so many wise men had tried to answer the question and failed, and he couldn't even get up the steps but had the impertinence to think he could answer. He then said, "I laughed because you take all this for real, but the only reality is the Self." The king understood, and although himself a realized man, became a pupil of Ashtavakra. King Janaka is famous for becoming a saint but remaining a king and continuing to carry out all his duties in the world like any householder.

Ashtavakra meant that all the king experienced in his dream was just as unreal (the dream, the real tears, and the throne) as this scene they were enacting at that moment.

THE INDIAN AND THE AFRICAN MONEYLENDER

The fear of death haunts the mind of even the bravest of people. Everybody, whether great or small, learned or ignorant, fears death, but in fact there is no such thing as death. So-called 'death' is nothing but a natural corollary of the phenomenon of birth. The only way to avoid death is to avoid being born. It is not possible to be born and not die.

Actually, the individual Self, living in the body, is immortal. It gives up an old body in order to put on a new body, just as we give up our old clothes and put on new ones. If we are happy to discard an old garment and put on a new one, there is no reason to be unhappy when the Self discards an old body and adopts a new one.

An Indian went to Africa. When his money ran out, he went to a moneylender to ask for a loan. Just then, there was a death in an Indian family living in that neighbourhood and the members of the family were weeping. The moneylender asked the

Indian why his countrymen were weeping. The Indian replied that it was a custom in his country to weep when there was a death in the family.

The moneylender asked again, "And what do you do when there is a birth in the family?" The Indian said, "Then we rejoice."

The moneylender said, "Then, if you are the sort of person who rejoices when receiving a thing but weeps when you have to return it, I certainly won't lend you any money!"

A person who dies has never written back to say what happens to him after death. Therefore, the only course open to us is to take the authority of the holy scriptures on subjects relating to death and the hereafter. We can find a lot of information there on these subjects. The following teachings from the *Bhagavad-Gita* tell us how to deal with death:

> Forget the past. Do not fear the future either. Devote the present to the worship of God. A devotee of God never perishes.
>
> For two half-hours a day, give up all duties and obligations; surrender yourself completely to the single care and protection of God. He will save you from all evil consequences and therein will lie the end of all your worries.
>
> If one sees God in everybody and everything, and sees everybody and everything in God, God never becomes obscure to such a person and he never becomes obscure to God.

We fear death because, under the influence of ignorance, we have forgotten our real Selves. And it is this forgetting of the divine Self which makes all our troubles for us. It is not God who is the maker of our troubles.

When one comes into this world one comes from some other world. Having lived one's life in this world, one must return to that other world, so from the universal realm, one comes at birth into the individual realm. When a person dies, that person is going back to the Father and it is a moment of rejoicing rather than of sorrow, because he is attaining the ultimate state.

One should not, then, feel grief at all when someone passes away, because he is going back to the real Father, though leaving the temporary and physical father and mother. We ought to console ourselves and keep our attention directed to the real Father of all, whose family is spread throughout the world. When somebody is called back, we should happily allow that person to go; if we were to keep on remembering him, we would be hurting that being because he would feel some attachment, some attraction to this life because of the grief we show.

Young or old, we should feel happy that one of His children has gone back to his real home. This universe is the travel ground—we have come here only for a little while.

THE TWO PEOPLE WHO WANTED TO BE DISCIPLES

Is the time-scale of the subtle body manifested on the physical level by man's architecture, works of art, and writings, because they all have a duration far longer than his physical body and seem to give a hint of this other time-scale? Can one extend this experience to a different understanding of the causal level?

The change in sense of time-scale is due to abundance of *sattva* (the quality or energy of purity and light). All creative work done by anyone starts when he is at peace—peace acquired only through *sattva*. If he is agitated, he can't paint; no painting is possible if you are not at peace. Agitation or laziness reduce the time-scale, and reduction of time-scale means reduction of creative work. Creative art is the means of showing as much as possible of the whole of creation and extends the time-scale. This is the real interest of the inner Self, so when you say you have observed a change in time-scale through man's legacy of architecture, writing, etc., they are certainly a result of this aspect of creativity.

The *Bhagavad-Gita* says that from consciousness and its contact with the world comes desire. If the desire is not fulfilled, then anger arises, and if anger does not fulfil the desire which was originally there, and there are further hindrances, then a bond is created between this man and his desire and he persists by hook or by crook to fulfil it. Because of this his mind gets agitated, the agitation of mind blocks his reason and when this happens the man is almost destroyed. From this you will see that if you can create more purity through feeling, by study, or by whatever means, then the peace will be there, there will be less agitation, and creative work will follow.

There was a holy man to whom two people went for advice to become disciples. Before accepting them he asked one of them to fill the water pot outside. This boy went and saw that it was more than half full of water. He returned to the holy man and said there was plenty of water in it, but he would certainly fetch fresh water when it was used up. The holy man asked the second one to go and fill the pot; he also saw that there was enough water, but he immediately took a bucket to the well, drew and filled it completely, and then returned and reported to the holy man and asked if they could begin work. The holy man refused to accept the first boy but accepted the second as a disciple.

If one can keep one's mind really open—open to good influences without any attachment to success or failure, without any agitation in the mind, or laziness in handling anything which comes before one in the course of one's daily life, then in spite of all the difficulties, one will keep on improving one's inner being and the world in which one lives. That is the way to live.

THE DEATH OF BALI IN THE *RAMAYANA*

When one has the feeling of the long time-scale of the subtle body which is so much greater in breadth and duration than the physical body, then it is easy to perform the actions without being involved, because they seem very limited, very small, and it is natural to drop them. I had this feeling that the subtle body was so much bigger than the physical body that the death of a physical body meant nothing.

This state is exactly the state where real love starts, when the love of the physical body ceases to exist then real love comes. Although the message is being given all the time, yet it is very difficult for people to transcend the love of the physical body. Although it is equally true that we love the physical not for the sake of the physical, but for the sake of the Self within the physical, yet somehow we get entangled and limit the whole thing to the physical body. Then when the pleasure of being in physical proximity is denied we feel sorry, but this sorrow is unnecessary—this is the hindrance to real love. Let real love flow and there should be no difficulty of communication with the beloved.

There is an example from the *Ramayana:*

At one stage a man called Bali was killed and his wife Tara felt very sad, and Rama, who was responsible for the death of this man, was there. He did not want to kill the man, nor give the woman grief, so he wanted to console her. He asked what it was that gave her so much sorrow, whom did she really love, who was the real man she wanted union with, was it the physical man she loved, the subtle man, or the true Self himself? So Tara had to think. Rama said that if she loved the physical man, he was still right in front of her, and she could still love him, but if she loved the true Self of this man, then as it was quite certain that the Self lived all the time everywhere, could she not see that his Self was within her Self? Was there no unity? Had she forgotten him? Tara understood the question and the situation. She said that she certainly loved the Self, not the body, and with this came the understanding that she had not lost her husband, only the living body which anyway had to go one day.

3

Discipline

THE PARENTS WHO QUARRELLED OVER THEIR UNBORN SON

I find that my mind is running either into the past or the future and does not make use of the present moment for Self-realization.

There was a lawyer who got married and after some time he and his wife started planning their future. The lawyer suggested that when they had a son, they should bring him up and educate him to be an even better lawyer than his father. The wife had something else in mind. She wanted her son to become a doctor because her parents were in the medical profession. Once the argument started it became very heated.

While they were arguing a holy man happened to appear and asked them why they were fighting. The husband stated his ambitions and the wife explained hers. The holy man asked them to call the boy and enquire as to what he would like to be, but the couple said, "The child is not yet born." The holy man laughed at this stupid planning even before the child was born. Such future plans have no substance. Such desires are not useful. Pure discrimination suppresses such foolish desires and

imaginings, like a snake-charmer who presses down any snake
that raises its head unnecessarily. Desires are not bad but too
many of them are bad and all superfluous imaginings are
useless.

THE GHOST AND THE BAMBOO POLE

*How can one improve the benefit of the meditation when one has trouble
with the moving mind coming and going during the half-hour?*

When one sits for the meditation in a still position there may
be distractions outside while one is trying to meditate, and these
distractions will attract the mind. One has to learn not to be distracted by outer influences.

Apart from outer distractions, there are internal riots! These
keep going on in the mind, which is drawn to certain things one
wants to do, and this is all the mind is doing—it is presenting
difficult files for your consideration. When you are almost still
you can give more energy to these files, so your mind tries to
help you to look at them. In fact, this is not the time for those
files, so make a resolution—tell the mind this is not the time:
"When I have finished my meeting with the Self, I will surely
attend to those files." Then you will attend to them later, and
resolve those questions which seem to be bothering the mind.
This is the way: order the mind and it will follow your commands, provided you do command it and make a resolution. Let
the mind stay at the gate, and ask it not to allow any files to be
presented to you now, you will see them later on. And do see
them later on.

Someone in pursuit of spiritual knowledge and practice turned to some sort of rituals in order to gain control of a ghost. He hoped to use it like a servant and get most of his work done by this ghost so that he would be free himself to meditate, study, and do spiritual work. Before the ghost had taken on the job it had said that if there was no work, it would devour the man! This was the condition—it had to be kept busy all the time! The man thought there was plenty to do, so the ghost could be kept busy like any other human being, but the ghost was very quick in completing the tasks and returning for more orders, and very soon it finished all the work the man could think of.

Now the man had an inspiration, and said to himself that with the quickness of this ghost it was impossible to give it enough jobs, so it should be given some job to which it must attend all the time which would never come to an end. He had an idea, and asked the ghost to cut a bamboo pole and bring it to him and fix it in the courtyard. When the ghost had fixed it firmly there, the man said, "Unless I ask you to come and do a special job, your general job is to go up and down this pole." Now, going continually up and down this pole exhausted the ghost very quickly, and then it settled down at the bottom of the pole to wait for the next order from his holy man.

The mind is very like a ghost; its job is to propose and counter-propose and there is no end to the variety of counter-propositions it can produce. This is the job of the mind and that is how it keeps people busy, and people get tired, not only mentally, but physically.

The pole is the mantra. Order the mind there, and it will settle down fairly quickly. There is no reason for the mind not to follow you, the mind always follows a command. If you command it to be peaceful, it will be peaceful. If your command is wavering, then you are not asking your mind to be peaceful.

At most one can do ten hours' work and take six hours' sleep. For the rest of the time one must employ the mind in useful work, i.e., in meditation, good company, study of good literature or scriptures. Use your discrimination to make your mind work for the Master, and do not allow the mind to establish a kingdom of its own in which to do what it wants. One must make an effort and use discrimination. Hard work is not bad. It is neither bad for the body, the mind, or the Self. It's only a question of direction. Hard work for what? Does one do it for use of the Self or for pleasure? Hard work for the Self will not do any harm.

You use a car to travel fast. When you reach your destination you stop the engine. The mind is like the engine. If you don't need to use it, then don't allow it to run for nothing. Just stop it, give it a rest, or give it some useful work.

Mind doesn't naturally run; it is encouraged to run. When your discrimination allows it to run, then it runs. A weak intelligence is overruled by it. Don't allow your intellect to be weak or impure. Fewer desires and no imaginings are good for progress. This keeps the mind in good form.

An idling engine uses up the battery, which then needs recharging. An idle mind uses all our energy and must be recharged. In meditation we recharge the energy, but why misuse it? Use it for a better purpose. Use it for the Self and then even the body and senses will get their share of real happiness. An overworked engine is always in danger of wearing out, an idle one of getting rusty. So one must find the means to use energy properly in a balanced way.

Some people while away their time in playing cards. These habits are neither useful in the material world nor the spiritual world. If one has to have habit, one should have a good habit. Although habits are no good for the Self, yet a good habit will at least put one on the better side of the fence.

The first of the Upanishads *(Isha Upanishad)* begins: "Whatever lives is full of the Lord. Claim nothing; enjoy, do not covet His property. Then hope for a hundred years of life doing your duty."

We are not asked to live a hundred years of misery. However, our life does become a life of misery because of our feeling of attachment to worldly things and this feeling of attachment to worthless things is the root of all miseries. The world, as it really is, has no miseries at all. It is we who manufacture them by harbouring an attachment to worldly things.

Attachment means, to consider as ours what really belongs to God, 'our body,' 'our house,' 'our wealth,' 'our son,' etc. Give up this feeling and you get rid of all troubles.

Do not think that the world around you, i.e. your house, your money, your body, etc., are insubstantial. Rather, it is your feeling of attachment to them which is insubstantial. Whatever is happening around you is right, but what is wrong about it is the view you are taking of it. If you could correct your viewpoint, you would be happy.

The world is a great show, which God is staging around you in the shape of the universe. But it is a mere show. Your birth is a show, your death is a show. Actually there is neither birth nor death. Know that, and you will be happy.

The common outlook is that the world is everything, and that the Absolute is nothing. It is wrong to hold this view, and the punishment for it is to be imprisoned in this physical body. You cannot be happy while undergoing a term of imprisonment.

Our mind has the property of thinking of something or other

all the time; it cannot remain idle. If it does not remember the Absolute, it will think of the world. Remembering the Absolute leads to happiness, and thinking of the world leads to unhappiness.

It is true that people do not find it easy to hold the Absolute in mind. The reason for that is lack of practice. As long as the ability has not been acquired, there will be difficulty. But the ability can certainly be acquired.

A baby cannot eat solid food in the beginning because the ability has not been acquired. But this ability comes quite easily later after he has some teeth.

Acquiring the ability to think of the Absolute is as easy as that. Keep the mind occupied like the mahatma's servant who was told to climb up and down the pole.

You have a mind, you have a body, and you have intelligence. Let the mind be trained to remember the Absolute, let the body serve Him, and let the intelligence discriminate.

The Disciple Who Fell into the Well

We should never allow the mind to establish its own imaginary kingdom of pleasure.

There was a disciple attending on a holy man. He used to go to the town to collect alms to buy food for them both. One day he saw a procession. On enquiring about it he was told that a girl and a boy were getting married and they would live together in love, peace, and happiness. Farther on he stopped by a well to rest and fell asleep. He dreamt and saw himself being married, taking his bride home, and being in bed with her. His wife asked him to move over a little which he did, and fell into the well. The people in the town got him out and asked what had happened. How had he fallen into the well in daylight? He told of his dream to the great amusement of the people, and went back to the hermitage, resolving not to allow the mind to create its own kingdom!

People fall into wells just for nothing!

THE MERCHANT WHO FELL ASLEEP

There was a cloth merchant who used to get very excited and was in the habit of thinking without purpose, imagining designs and so on. One of his well-wishers took him to a meeting. There he sat in the back row and due to complete lack of interest he was soon fiddling with the shirt of the person sitting in front of him. Later on he fell asleep and dreamt he was selling his cloth. After discussions with a client in the dream, he was asked to tear off a piece of cloth a few yards in length. Having heard this the fiddling fingers got busy and tore the shirt of the person sitting in front of him, which woke him up and he opened his eyes to see what he had done. The other man was furious. The merchant promised to give him six yards of new cloth and begged him not to make a fuss. He then also realized the futility of idle thoughts.

DO EVERYTHING FOR GOD

A mahatma was approached by an ordinary man and asked what he should do—he did not feel he could undergo much discipline, so what was the simplest way? The mahatma said he could find the Absolute if he just kept running, and when he fell exhausted he would find the Absolute.

The man asked, "If the Absolute can be found by running, why not just by sitting?" "Yes," he replied, "perhaps by sitting, but the question is, what are you sitting for? If you are sitting for the Absolute, He will meet you, if you are running for the Absolute, He will meet you in that. You can do anything, it does not really matter; the real crux is whether you are doing it for the sake of the Absolute or for some worldly end." The mahatma continued by saying that the unity with the Absolute is already there, nobody has to acquire it, but because we have all forgotten our unity, we are only required to give up our ignorance, give up our forgetfulness by any method.

All the different yogas (there are hundreds of them) lead in only one direction, but the individual who wants to go by any of these ways has to decide once and for all that whatever he does, he does for the Absolute, and then he will find this union.

If you try to do anything, however wonderfully you may do it, if it is just to fulfil your worldly commitments, then you will find that the union which is already there will not be experienced, so the thing to decide is that one is doing everything—even digging the earth or anything else one chooses to do—for the Absolute.

In the *Bhagavad-Gita* it says that "people should take to this through their own vocation; whatever they are destined to do or whatever they find themselves already doing is good enough," and that is the way, that is the yoga for unity with the Absolute. The only thing is that everything must be done for the Absolute, and nothing should be done to acquire any particular thing except union with the Absolute. One should just surrender oneself, and the feeling of surrender itself is the gate of liberation; a devotee is always liberated because he is not bothered about anything except the Absolute. A devotee does not necessarily undergo discipline; he simply lives a liberated life.

Suppose a householder has four children; the eldest has finished his education, done his training, got a job, and is bringing in some money for the general family maintenance. The next child has passed his examinations, but has not yet enrolled in service or employment, and the third is still studying. The fourth one is not even old enough to go to school, so he is just playing around and enjoying himself. If one wanted to know which of the four was most loved by his father, it would seem very difficult to decide, but nevertheless if one tried to decide one would say that the youngest was getting most of his father's love. Because he is helpless, he does not contribute anything, he is not even clever enough to recite anything learnt at school— and yet he is loved the most. The mother loves him, and whenever the father comes home and is given food, the little boy sits on his lap and gets fed by the father. Sometimes the boy picks up one or two pieces of food and puts them into his father's mouth in response to all that is being done for him. This little offering of a small child fills the father with the greatest joy of his life.

In the same way the Absolute is father of all in this universe, and whether one is incapable of doing anything, whether one is learned, whether one is earning anything or not, whether one is about to earn to repay the debt, it doesn't matter: He loves all of us.

Draupadi (the daughter of King Drupada in the great Indian epic the *Mahabharata*) and some other devotees are very like children—this is the quality they show. The acts which they perform are those which one usually associates with a servant who is thoroughly devoted to serving his master's needs day and night.

On one occasion Draupadi gave a holy man a very small piece of cloth. Then occurred the episode when she was being dragged into court to be stripped by one of the Kauravas. That little piece of cloth came to her rescue. Her sari grew longer and longer until those who wanted to undress her grew tired and gave up the attempt. So her honour was saved just by that tiny strip of cloth.

The Absolute is very like an ocean of love which is available to everyone, but because of ignorance people do not realize the availability of this ocean of love and keep on hankering after the world and worldly things. If only people came to know the ocean of bliss and love, and if they could acquire just one drop of this their lives would be fulfilled.

People from all parts of India come to the Ganges. It is flowing all the time, but at certain times these people come from far and wide: they take a dip in the Ganges and collect the water in small pots, and they keep this Ganges water with them for the year, till they come next time. Whenever they have to perform any sacrifice or similar work, they use a little of the Ganges water and they feel they are united and that everything is purified for them, and it gives them great pleasure. So one only has to realize that the Absolute is everywhere, His love is available to everyone, and if only one could attach oneself to Him entirely, surrender to Him, everything would be possible.

THE OLD WOMAN WHO STOLE THE CLOCK

What I seem to need in order to transform both the meditation half-hours and my daily life is love and faith. Last year you quoted the prayer of the great poet, Tulasidas: "Please by your grace let my nature be pure and with complete balance. Only then will I be able to worship you!" This is my own prayer as well.

Many people who get to know something about truth or goodness are drawn towards it and try to improve. They begin to attend the ashram. Some are more sincere than others, but governed by their nature and habits they go on making the same mistakes again and again. Some take to discipline and practise austerities, perform rituals and meditate, but when the real time to stand by the truth or discipline comes, they give way to their nature and fall. They repent, pray for forgiveness, even shed tears, undergo penance, and do the same again. Such is their nature.

In Dehradun, in an ashram, an old woman of eighty used to go for *satsang* (a spiritual meeting). She would immerse herself in worship and chanting, do all the other work of the ashram, seemed a good devotee and was treated as such. But from childhood she had a habit of stealing. One day she stole the alarm clock and then pretended to search, expressed horror at whoever had stolen it, and made such a fuss that no one suspected that she was the thief. Anyway, the meeting started and very soon the alarm went off. She was right in the front row and the clock was recovered from her handbag!

Such people are plentiful for they are everywhere. However much practice and discipline they carry out, things revert to the same point. Change is possible only when there is a real desire for it; there must arise one paramount desire for truth which will permeate a person's nature and transform it. A real desire is something for which one would not stop anywhere short of fulfilment.

Nature, being the basis of the individual, is the most subtle of all causes of motivation. The coarse and subtle aspects of our life can be erased by 'disciplines' of the physical or intellectual kind, but to remove the most subtle nature hidden very deep in our being is, of course, very hard. This is that very deep desire which springs up only at odd moments when we are perhaps not too vigilant. This alone is the cause of all those disciples not experiencing real bliss in their devotional work. Here reason fails, but a strong desire can succeed.

A patient may be attended by a good doctor and good medicine may be prescribed together with a regulated diet and all the rest, but if the patient secretly manages to fall for a taste which he can't resist, then all this work will be useless. Here only the patient can help himself, by a strong desire to take regularly the medicine which will help him. Unless he conquers himself, no other outer agency can be of much use, like our story of the millionairess who used to eat sweets and never got cured. (See "The Millionairess Who Had Diabetes.")

Having come to the conclusion that there is a strong love for a certain thing which keeps us away from the purification of our nature, if the individual can't do it himself, although he wants to and works for it, and yet can't, then can any other agency be helpful in this matter?

All possible help can be given up to the limit of intellect or discrimination, but this problem lies beyond that and is close to the Self. All impulses and emanations of the Self start from that point and are affected by it. Outer help stops beyond the intellect; there the individual is alone; he must drop the craving himself. No other agency can do anything there, not even Grace. Only one's own Self is there.

THE MONKEY IN THE TREE

Most people meet two types of obstacles. One consists of the shortcomings in themselves, in their being, and the other is the fickleness of the mind. These are the two main things which have to be removed before one can make progress.

Somebody wanted to become Self-realized and went to a teacher who asked him what he saw on the way. The man described how he saw a monkey sitting under a tree. It climbed up the tree when he approached and then made some offensive gestures. The teacher asked him to get the monkey out of his mind, to contemplate anything but the monkey. The man found he couldn't do that at all.

I used to repeat this story of the Shankaracharya's as a joke, but lately I have seen that this monkey consists largely of what my personality is most proud of. I no longer feel safe with this monkey, and I would like to ask the Shankaracharya if he would be good enough to shoot him, or at least send him back to the jungle where he belongs!

The story of the monkey has a general feel about it. Everyone who aspires to rise high or go on the way towards liberation, wants Self-realization first and only after Self-realization might he wish to do the work! This process of thinking is wrong, for there is nothing like Self-realization now and work later!

When the aspirant expressed his inability to get the monkey out of his mind, the holy man pointed out that this is the nature of our existence, that whatever is taken in by the mind stays there. In a way the mind becomes whatever it observes, or one can say that the mind itself becomes the monkey and keeps old habits. This is how our experiences reduce our own being. One becomes whatever one takes in.

The way to get rid of all this is through the way of knowledge by which one sees things as they are; by meditation one reduces the effect of all one's habits, so as to allow the mind to work under the control of the Self. There are many such monkeys within each individual which have taken up their abode during the journey through innumerable lives, and they rise on occasion to disturb one's peaceful existence. They will play around as long as one allows them to play. To check all this one needs discipline.

THE DONKEY IN THE ROAD

At a certain stage in the development of meditation there seems to be a barrier blocking final unity. Is this illusion? If so, can one destroy it? If not, how can one overcome the barrier?

The last barrier to the Self is ego, the feeling of 'I': "I am the one who is meditating," or "I am the one who is about to transcend the barrier to unity." As long as one sticks to this, unity is impossible. One has to learn this and make sure in one-self that when one reaches this stage, one will drop even the idea of the feeling of I. Only when the sense or feeling of I is given up is unity possible.

A certain man went to a holy man to be initiated in medit-ation. He was asked what things he saw on the way. He said that among all the things he saw he remembered a donkey very well. He was then asked to remove the donkey from his memory. The poor man tried hard, but failed, and expressed his inability to do so. The holy man said that the art is to drop the memory. This memory or the feeling of I is the greatest and the last barr-ier to meditation. The man who meditates or the man who ob-serves must be dropped so that he is able to merge into one.

THE DHOBI MAN AND THE DONKEYS

One should never allow the moving mind to go free. It is a very important link in our being, so it must always be under control of our intelligence and power of discrimination. The body is eas-ily trained and that can be made free after a period of discipline. One can, of course, have some trials and tests to find out the level of one's mind and discrimination, and in order to find out one has to allow them a little freedom. If they naturally incline towards activities useful to the Self, then they can qualify for freedom, but not before. Schoolboys are given freedom to write what they feel in exams and thus their level is determined. One of the easy tests relates to one's dreams. In dreams people are mostly in their natural state of mind and the type of dream can reveal the workings of the mind.

One always has to be on the alert and not allow everything to happen by chance. The way of development needs attention and discipline. If one has lost the opportunity of discipline or the company of good men, one may suffer indefinitely. The human form is the platform where discipline is available; miss your chance and you continue repeating the same mistakes. The mind thinks that the world is true and likes to live with it in ignorance. This is illusion and to cure this illusion discipline is prescribed. Now even this discipline shouldn't be taken as reality. The truth is that one really is the Self and the Absolute, but one doesn't know this secret because of ignorance. Once you realize your real Self, the discipline also becomes unnecessary. If you have a thorn in your foot, you take it out with the help of another thorn and throw both thorns away after use! So in some way even the discipline is illusion, but only this illusion will undo the fundamental illusion of ignorance.

There was a *dhobi* (washerman), who used many donkeys to carry his load. One day he fell ill and asked his son to load the donkeys and take them with the washing. The boy loaded them and tried to move them towards the river but they would not budge an inch. Seeing they weren't tied up at all, he was surprised at what happened and went to ask his father who said, "Oh, I should have told you, in the evening I touch their feet as if I am trying to bind them with a rope, and in the morning touch them again as if I have undone them." The boy also did this, and then each donkey started to move. The fact is that the donkeys all thought they were not freed and therefore they could not walk. This is the condition of all human beings. The ignorance is illusory and to remove this one must undergo another illusion in order to realize one's real state; this is essential and we cannot evade it.

The Absolute creates the creation when looking outward. When looking within no creation takes place. So the creation becomes manifest and in this way body, mind, and intellect become manifest, too. Discipline turns one towards the 'within.' In the Self it is all bliss, consciousness, and truth.

TULASIDAS AND THE LOVE OF HIS WIFE

Discipline can be a spiritual activity. It is more like a medicine which gives happiness. In everyday life at all pressing moments it acts as a tonic to strengthen one with happiness, peace, and contentment.

When one experiences happiness as a result again and again, then one becomes sure that there must be a source or ocean of bliss from which one has been deriving the moments of happiness. With that little discipline when you get moments of real bliss and peace you will come nearer to the source through the discipline and you may also merge in that bliss; then no profit or loss in the material world will leave any mark. The stories are told to encourage and show the way to the source of bliss.

Tulasidas (who translated the *Ramayana* from Sanskrit into Hindi) was very much in love with his wife. He was so attached to her that he could not live a day without her. Once she went to her mother's home while Tulasidas was out. When Tulasidas didn't find her at home he went to look for her in her parents' house. He reached it at midnight and knocked on the door. His wife came out and teased him saying that if he loved God, who is all bliss, consciousness, and truth, as much as he loved her, he would certainly have complete liberation! This admonishment went deep into his heart and he immediately turned back home. Later he became a saint through his love of God.

ARJUNA AND THE EYE OF THE BIRD

In order to learn to do, you have first to learn to listen very exactly. Ordinary men do not have the capacity to attend accurately to instructions. To illustrate this, here is a story from the *Mahabharata:*

Before the great war was declared, all the warriors were being taught by Dronacharya, the instructor. He was teaching them the art of fighting. One day he instructed them to shoot at the eye of a bird which he hung on a tree. One by one he called them and said, "Mark the eye of the bird and get ready to shoot"; then he asked them what they saw. One said, "I see the branch and the face of the hanging bird, feathers, mouth, eyes, everything." He was dismissed. The next said, "I see the bird, neck, feathers, eyes," and he was told to go.

And so it was with everybody, until Arjuna stood there and, taking aim, was asked, "What do you see?"

He replied, "I see only the eye!"

"But don't you see anything else?"

"Nothing at all."

"Then go ahead and shoot"—and his arrow went straight into the eye of the bird. In listening, and in meditation, perfect attention is necessary.

4

Desires

THE MAN AND HIS PARROT

There are those who only like to know but do not put the knowledge into practice, and for such people the world is nothing more than talk. These are very poor creatures. Then there are those who only like to experience and care nothing about knowledge; they are filled with doubt when they meet with forceful opposition or bad company. Their faith is shaken and they stop practising. Thus a happy combination is very healthy, because one can taste the bliss of being and also remain strong in the face of false ideas and thus keep on the Way.

There was a man who was interested in listening to a saintly teacher, but never bothered to practise his instructions. His talking parrot once asked him where he went each day. He replied that he liked to know about God and liberation, etc., so he went to hear a saintly man. The parrot requested him to ask the saint on his behalf, "How can I be liberated?" The man put the question to the saint and the saint immediately fell down as if suddenly unconscious. People were very angry with the man for having put such an awkward question and asked him to leave at once. When the man came home he told the whole story to the parrot. The next morning the parrot was found lying motionless in his cage. His master took him to be dead and opened the cage to remove him. The parrot immediately flew up to a branch of a tree and said, "I got the saint's message and now I am free. It would be good for you if you had acted on the instructions given."

We decided that we should really try to practise what you teach, instead of merely thinking and talking about it! After the peace of meditation I had a feeling that something in my heart was free from its cage and up in a tree, like the parrot in the story, while its owner on the ground could not understand it at all.

Desires, which are always present in human beings—this is the nature of things—usually end up in attachment. Attachment comes because there are continuous associations between certain types of desires and the objects of those desires. If you go on being attached for longer, attachment becomes greed so that you always like to have things in plenty for an unlimited time. They go beyond your individual needs and this is craving or addiction. Greed and craving constitute the cage in which the individual ego is imprisoned. It is only possible to get out of prison if there is somebody to help. One can fall very easily into a well, but it is not possible to get out by oneself, even if one desperately wants to, unless someone on the surface is ready and able to help. So one needs guidance and leadership. For those who are intelligent, the scriptures, discourses, and certain words of the realized man will help.

So it is necessary for anyone seeking liberation to find a true teacher who will look after the ways and means.

You have said that attachment to desires is the cage, and people sometimes ask if the story of the parrot relates to the situation of the Self? But surely the Self is perfect?

The Self is never bound by anything, but the soul or inner organ, with its four parts of mind which we feel as 'I,' is superimposed on the Self. This is everyone's usual state but even then the Self is just as free as ever. In fact it is not the Self who is in a cage!

No. It feels like the emotional centre being freed—it is felt in the heart emotionally and then it lights up many of the things you have been saying.

The superimposition is caused by attachment, greed and addiction, and it seems that the inner organ itself gets into the cage because of these three. So the four parts of the mind are either free from those attachments, or they are in the cage due to them.

Under no circumstances is the real Self bound by anything, it is only the psyche. Those who seem to be liberated, or have no cage, experience freedom. Those who are not free are bound by their own desires, attachments and greed.

THE MAHATMA'S DREAM

In one of the scriptures it says: "This body is only flesh and bones; cease to be attached to it." Transfer your attachment to the Self. Because Self is part of the Universal Self, there is no difference between the two. Both are able to cut worldly bondage.

This body is the vehicle and the Self is the driver. Treat the driver separately from the vehicle. It is not easy to do so. It requires years of practice. We practise by thinking this body is God's property, not ours. This mind is God's property, not ours; everything is God's, and nothing is ours. In this way we free ourselves from all attachments, all constraints. Again, this concept is difficult for those who think that 'I' is the physical body.

A mahatma wished to live in complete solitude, in order that he could meditate undisturbed at all times. He repeated his wish to a rich man. The rich man had an isolated rest-house deep in the forest, rarely visited by anyone. He offered it to the mahatma, and in addition provided a young servant to look after his comfort.

The mahatma was so well looked after by the young servant that his heart was moved. He asked the young servant if he was content with his life, and if he, the mahatma, could do anything to bring him happiness. The young man replied that he himself was content and happy, but he was afraid that his dead father had not achieved Self-realization as he was frequently appearing in his dreams. He asked the mahatma for a remedy.

During the ensuing nights, the mahatma was haunted by the problem of the young man's father. One evening the boy went to a neighbouring village to attend a marriage feast, telling the mahatma that he would not return until the following morning. The mahatma locked up the house and went to bed. Now, the young servant's empty bed was beside that of the mahatma. The mahatma's mind was filled with thoughts about the young man's father, and his failure to achieve Self-realization. He was quite unable to sleep peacefully. The marriage feast was over by midnight, so the boy returned to the house immediately instead of waiting until the morning. When he got back, he climbed over the wall and through the window and fell asleep on his own bed.

At three-thirty in the morning, the mahatma awoke and saw the bed was occupied. In the darkness, he thought that the occupant must be the boy's father who had been haunting his son's dreams. He recited holy mantras and sprinkled blessed water over the body but the boy did not wake up as he was in such a deep sleep. So the mahatma became very frightened. He opened the window and jumped out in order to escape. In his haste, he fell over with a heavy thud. The noise awakened the young servant who chased after the mahatma with a heavy staff thinking that he was a burglar escaping. Eventually they recognised each other before many blows were sustained, and the misunderstanding was cleared up.

In such a way, just a momentary thought, stealing unconsciously into the mind, will make its home there, then it appears later at some inopportune moment to cause much mischief. Reels and reels of such thoughts from the past are lying printed on our minds. They will not let us have peace, unless we develop the same attachment towards God as we now have towards the world.

Our desires are like so many strings that pull us towards the world. Let this pull be towards God instead. The method is to establish the attitude that everything, including one's physical body and mind, belongs to God. Whatever actions we do, including eating, drinking, reading, writing, and looking after our duties, should all be dedicated to God.

This is the meaning of *Bhakti*, the path of devotion. Done in this way, each and every action of yours becomes an act of devotion and so becomes an act of worship to God, instead of being a worldly act. The worldly ties are then broken and the presence of God supervenes. In the absence of such a way of thinking, there is only the world, and with the world come all our troubles!

RAMA AND THE BOATMAN

If the desire is good, then it takes the individual nearer the Absolute, but if the desire is wrong and bad, then it takes the individual away from the Absolute, so he becomes far removed, according to the extent of his bad desires. What does one really want? Does one want one's own desire to take one away from the Absolute or nearer to Him? That one will have to decide.

If one has chosen to go nearer to the Absolute, then one will have to respond to good desires. One doesn't have to go far to know what a good desire is, because the individual is made in such a way that, immediately after a desire arises, there is something within which always prompts one, and decides whether such a desire is right or wrong for oneself, one doesn't have to ask anyone. But because either one is in a great hurry to override this call from within, or one decides to go away from the Absolute, one doesn't respond to this prompting.

One just has to realize, to see, that the desire of the Absolute is a desire common to all. For instance, everybody in the world wants knowledge, whether he is English, American, German, or Indian, that makes no difference, because it is in the nature of the will of the Absolute that every individual must receive knowledge, so everyone wants it.

Then, again, everybody wants true knowledge; there isn't anyone, any sect in the world, which doesn't want truth. Their ideas and concepts about truth may differ, but they all seek it and truth itself cannot differ.

One can take the example of addition—two plus two makes four. The name of four may differ, or the word for two may differ, but the answer to 'two plus two' will never differ anywhere in any language, in any nation or in any creed.

So there are basic human things which everyone wants; likewise there is always some basic agreement. This agreement is the balance, and this balance is universal. If only people could see that there is a balance, and that something within one responds to this; if one could listen and follow one's own true prompting, one would certainly not go wrong. But people try to reason in such a way as to justify their wrong view, and they may promise to correct it later but meantime they do wrong. The ultimate way to have true knowledge of right and wrong is either from within, or from the application of reason which comes from the purified intellect.

Why, oh why is it so difficult to know what one wants? What is the longing in the heart, the sense of something lacking, the discontent, and upon what should we centre our minds and hearts to bring the answer or resolve the conflict?

There was an incident in Ayodhya, the capital of Rama's kingdom. Rama went to cross the Saraya River, but the boatman refused to take him. There is a lot of mythology attached to this passage in the *Ramayana*, and this boatman became very famous because of this episode.

A holy man wanted to cross that river some time ago. Suddenly he remembered the story of that boatman and Rama. He was so overwhelmed by the memory of the boatman that he said to this boatman: "Today, I will give you whatever you want."

The boatman answered very quickly, "Please arrange for today's meal." The holy man laughed, and wondered why, when this boatman was offered anything, whatever he wanted, all he asked for was the next meal! Then, in his wonderment, he realized that the poor man had no vision beyond his daily bread; if he had a wider vision he would have asked for more. So, in fact, he couldn't be blamed; he could not ask for a thing he didn't know. And he was given what he wanted.

THE RICH MAN AND HIS ADOPTED SON

A child only wants to play with toys; when he grows up, he wants books and other things. Later, he grows tired of books, and enters some other field of activity. Then he gets married, and things keep on changing from age to age and year to year. Unless a man reaches a state where he wants the real truth, where he wants truth, consciousness and bliss and he has to have it, he cannot make progress.

In Delhi there was a rich man who couldn't have children, so he adopted a boy from the same caste. After the adoption ceremony he took this boy to a car salesroom in the main shopping centre of Delhi. The boy was shown all sorts of large and grand cars of every description. But the boy asked for the smallest car there, though he was warned that only two could sit in it, and he wouldn't be able to take his mother nor many passengers, and so was advised to have a bigger car. He insisted that he wanted the small one, and said it would suit him, and so he was given it.

In two years' time he realized that it was too small and asked for a bigger one, which he was given. After some time, he asked for a still larger car as he needed one suitable for several passengers, and again he was given it.

In fact, life is a journey of appreciation of what one really wants, and it comes only from the level of knowledge and being which one has reached. One cannot fabricate the real question; one just has to wait.

People can be given knowledge and the Advaita system through which they may come to the ultimate question a little more quickly. But they have to take each step themselves and come to that final question, the truth about the Self.

Two Kinds of Suffering

There are two types of disease, or perhaps two types of the effect of disease: one is pain caused by physical illness, and the other is suffering like grief or sorrow which may come through the physical illness. This suffering may arise without a disease, because a number of people are seen to be suffering without any obvious disease of their body (or without any obvious lack in their life, for they seem to have everything), yet they still live in misery.

Physical disease certainly has its pain, just because it is physical, but this pain can be multiplied and increased with the addition of sorrow which is internal; that is, mental and emotional suffering. So one can increase or decrease the effect of physical pain. There are examples of people who, having had physical pain, did not become full of misery, so the physical pain came and, without much effect, left them when it was due to go.

Ramakrishna had cancer of the throat, and he was offered medicine which he refused. He said, "I am not grieving at all. The pain of the disease is there so I may cry out sometimes, but this does not really produce any grief in me. I am as happy as I can be, so I will endure this."

A similar episode occurred in the life of the great poet, Tulasidas. He also had some physical trouble, and he used to go for his daily bathe, passing through the Shiva temple in Benares. The trouble went on for two months.

After two months someone told him of a particular herb which he could apply to produce a very quick cure for this trouble. Tulasidas said he had had his trouble for two months without any solution being offered to him. Now, after this length of time, medicine was being offered, but perhaps the disease was about to end. He did not take the medicine, and the disease, having fulfilled its cycle, vanished.

Pain produces comparatively little suffering. If one can help to relieve people professionally from physical pain, that is good. But the greatest and most extensive pain arises from sorrow, which is internal. A greater service to humanity would be fulfilled if some remedy were given on this level as well as on the physical.

THE OLD LADY WHO ASKED FOR
TOO MANY THINGS

What is the function of desire?

Desires are not independent; mostly they are connected with your previous tendencies, but some new desires also arise because of present associations. For instance, a man is standing in the road and a very good car passes by. Instantaneously he feels like owning one himself—a desire arises. Now if he has money then probably he will be able to fulfil that desire, otherwise it will just remain a futile desire in his mind.

There was an old lady who happened to come here. She was blind. She had four sons. The first thing she said to me was: "Sir, do something by which I might get back my sight," and a minute after, she said, "I've got four sons, my second son has no child. Can you bless my son with a child?" Then she said, "The two wives of two of my sons don't obey me. Kindly do something that they may be obedient." Then again she said, "My eldest son is not doing well in business. Can you shower your blessings on him so that he may do better?" In this way she recounted about seven or eight desires, one after the other. I heard her patiently, and ultimately said, "Look here, you are on the verge of death, why don't you ask, 'Kindly let the Lord do something by which He may have pity on me and may do something by which I may achieve the purpose of my life and be happier hereafter.' You have asked for so many things; all these things are not possible. If you had asked for only one thing, then it would probably have been possible to help you. But to help you in getting all those circumstances you desire, that is not possible."

Similarly, when we have many desires, the Lord will find it very difficult to fulfil all of them, and actually many of those desires are not exactly essential. If desire is associated with your previous tendencies and habits one should want to be free of them. If it is a new desire it will create new tendencies. There will be less chance of creating new tendencies if you have fewer desires. It is not possible to say you have no desire, since you have been given this birth as a result of your previous tendencies. In order to reap the results of these habits, you must have certain desires; the effort should be to limit the desires so that you do only the reaping, not the sowing.

5

Discrimination

THE TWO ANTS

How can one help others intensify their desire for Self-realization?

Every human being looks for happiness. It is natural for him
to do this. If he gets a taste of it he wants more; again this is
natural. Anyone who has made even a little progress and who
has taken to meditation must have had at least some taste of it.
Two things can be done to encourage the taste further, and also
to attract those who have not yet experienced the taste. First,
by example. If people see you leading a productive life and see
that you are in a good and peaceful state, they will be attracted.
They will want to know what you have got and they will ask.
The second thing is to tell them of the knowledge you have
been given and explain it. If you drop grains of sugar here and
there, ants will follow the trail till they reach the source. Once
anyone gets a glimpse of it they will not forget it and will want
more. So the efficiency with which you deliver the message and

your personal example will be the grains of sugar which will bring people to Self-realization.

There were two mountains and there were ants living on each; one was a mountain of sugar and the other of salt. One day an ant from the sugar mountain went to visit an ant on the mountain of salt. After trying the salt which was not to her taste, she said to the other ant: "Why don't you come up to my place? Then you will see what delicious food is available there." So, the salt-fed ant went to the other mountain, but, not being sure of getting enough good food, she took some along in reserve and held a particle of salt in her mouth. So when she ate the sugar, because she had salt in her mouth, she said, "I don't find much difference between your stuff and mine." Then the other ant said, "Perhaps you are holding something of your own within. Get rid of that and I am sure you will see for yourself that the taste of my food is good." When she did this the salt-fed ant never went back to her mountain of salt again.

It is the same with human beings; even if we are offered the sugar of true knowledge, we will not taste its true flavour if we retain the craving for the salt of material things and worldly desires. Remove this salt and enjoy the pure sweetness of sugar, then you will want nothing else.

If you scatter grains of sugar on the ground leading to the store, an ant will follow the grains to the store. One who wants peace and bliss will collect grains of peace and bliss and follow the trail to full consciousness and bliss.

THE SERVANT WHO PRETENDED TO BE
A HOLY MAN

Stressing the need for constant practice in meditation, His Holiness once gave learning to ride a bicycle as an example. Sometimes when a boy is having difficulty in learning, a grown-up will hold him steady. In meditation can help be given in this way?

Two worlds are concerned here, the coarse physical world and the subtle world. All the direct help which one can give is in the physical world. So when somebody is trained in meditation he is told how to start the mantra, what to do, not to move one's body, to close one's eyes, and these are all physical things. This is all that can be given as far as the physical body is concerned. In the realm of the subtle body, indications or directions can be given, but these directions have to be carried out by the meditator himself. Beyond this it is impossible to do anything.

Meditation is a journey back home, and most of the troubles and tribulations which one experiences are in the first half of the journey; when that point is passed and you are nearer home, then there is only one point to look for and you don't have to bother about anything else. Meditation is going back home—home to the Self. What the teacher can do is to describe the journey from start to finish and show what usually happens and what may be met on the way.

In the realm of mind the teacher can guide and tell the disciple to attend to the mantra, and if the mind does not behave properly the teacher can help on the level of the intellect and discrimination by referring to knowledge, giving all the information of what is usually experienced so that the disciple can investigate and discriminate by himself. But when the journey back home starts, this discrimination has to be done by the disciple himself, to discriminate what comes from the causal body and what are outer influences. He does not have to stop and enquire, but go direct to the Absolute or Self. It is only up to the disciple, no help is possible on this level.

When a secret meeting is arranged, the person who makes the arrangements leads people only so far, and beyond that he does not go, but leaves the people to meet by themselves. The same applies to a husband and wife; although they have many relatives and so on, when they want to have an intimate conversation, they do not want anyone else present. It is in the nature of the Self that when it turns back to itself, by its own nature it does not want anyone's interference or help, and since it does not want help, there is no possibility and no need to give it. In the scriptures it has been said that on the way to liberation even discrimination has a limit. Beyond this the Self experiences itself.

When during meditation one tastes the inner happiness which is not available in the physical world, then one wants to have it again and again. In the same way you can drop a few grains of sugar but you do not have to create a road for the ant to travel from one grain to another. Once it has tasted the sugar the ant will find its way to the next grain. It is the same for oneself. Once one tastes the inner happiness, then one does not need anyone's help because one is capable of making the journey oneself.

This is the story of the king who asked his minister to bring him a holy man so that he could learn the secret of eternal wealth. The minister could not find a really holy man, so he instructed his servant how to pretend to be one. When the king was satisfied, the servant was instructed to resume his normal duties but he preferred to continue to practise being a holy man in order that he could meet the greatest of all kings.

The moral of this story is that one can be led to a certain point, but beyond that limit the journey is made by the Self without anybody's help, because the Self knows everything and it is only because it lives in the dark that it has forgotten its great potential.

THE MAN WHO WANTED TO MEET GOD

The Absolute is the root and cause of everything and of itself. In the cycle of cause and effect all manifestations have their place in relation to their forms. If one goes on seeking the chain of cause and effect, ultimately one reaches the Absolute, which is itself causeless. Thus the basis of all the names and forms is the consciousness of the Absolute.

So on the way discrimination is necessary between these forms and elements and the pure Self, and this must take place whether in meditation or when going about our affairs?

We naturally live in the world of names and forms and we are surrounded by them, and even the being we call ourself has many names and forms. People have name, form, and also the Self; thus it seems everything is everywhere, but because of ignorance people get involved in only the world of name and form. Usually they take their six-foot body as their ultimate being. The Advaita system of knowledge and the method of meditation is to remove the narrowness of the boundary and bondage, and allow people to discriminate and see the unlimited, unbounded Self, which cannot be limited by names and forms. Here is an example:

Someone went to a holy man and asked to be introduced to God. The holy man said, "When I go to Him, He will ask about you. What shall I say about you? So first give me some details of your own credentials." The man pointed to his body and told his name. The holy man said, "All this is made of flesh and bones which are always subject to growth and decay. How could this be you? It is only your body and name. Give me your proper credentials." The man thought and said that perhaps his thoughts, desires, and feelings were his proper credentials. The holy man again observed, "These are changing all the time even more rapidly than the bodily form. Give me your proper and fixed credentials." In this way this man was led to recognise his own true Self, and then he did not seek any more introductions.

The Advaita system of knowledge and method of meditation are simply to lead people to discriminate between the transitory and the eternal, between inner and outer, between words and the Spirit, so that one can enjoy forms and words, and also the real being.

TEN MEN CROSSING THE RIVER

In the world today there are a multitude of ideas prevailing, and everybody stands up to declare his principles and wants to lead

everybody else according to his own principles; others are also trying to state their own! In this situation there is, of course, need
for a man who is not involved in any desire for ideological victory.

Ten men were crossing a fast river and when they reached
the other side they started counting themselves to make sure
that all had reached the other side safely. Each one counted but
found only nine because he did not count himself, and they became very worried. Just at that time a holy man passed by and
looking at their miserable faces asked what was wrong; they told
him and demonstrated how there were only nine of them,
though they had started as ten. He made them stand in line and
with his stick he hit the first man once and separated him from
the line. He hit the second one twice, and so on till the last one.
He hit him ten times and declared he was the tenth one. They
were very happy and went on their way.

The same situation today prevails in the world. These ten
men represent the numerous ideologies which prevail, each
counting all the others without looking at itself, so they all like
to keep on fighting. Unless somebody else comes along and hits
each of them hard to bring them to their senses, this situation
will go on.

The Holy Man's Advice to the Snake

*It seems that when we let the ego interfere with our role in life, it's then
that we distort the play.*

One cannot do anything without the involvement of ego,
but there are different types of ego.

For instance, one can be angry, but there are two ways of being angry. With real anger the body of the angry man starts burning all over. But if the anger is only a part of the play, if it is only to provide a reprimand in a situation which needs correction, and if it is only outward, but with love inside, then this show of anger may be necessary, and it is useful if it does not start burning one up.

In that way ego is also useful provided it does not disturb the individual; if it is only for use in a certain situation it is all right, but if it is for the destruction of the Self then it is not right.

A number of holy men were going through a forest and they happened to see a large snake. They realized that, owing to misdeeds, some person had been turned into this snake, so they took some water from their pots and with the help of a mantra they sprinkled this over the snake, and the snake was turned back into a human form. This man told the holy men that in a previous life he had troubled quite a number of people and the result of all his sins was that he was turned into a snake. He begged the holy men to advise him how to escape from this situation. The holy men said the cure was not to trouble anyone any more, so, while a snake, he should not bite anyone, and if he did this, in the course of time he would be liberated. They then went on their way.

This man, in the form of a snake, stopped biting anyone. Slowly all the villagers, who used to come to collect fruit or wood or anything from the jungle and who always threw stones at him, found that this did not disturb him, there was no reaction, so they started coming closer and the stones hit him. Even then nothing happened, so they took some sticks and started beating him, and pulled his tail, and dragged him all over the place. All sorts of trouble befell this snake, but because he had promised not to bite he kept quiet and endured his sufferings.

After a number of months the holy men were returning through the same forest and saw this same snake lying there with all his bruises, and they asked what was happening to him. He said their advice was not to take action against anybody and he had followed their advice to the letter and this was the result because everyone attacked him. So the holy men said they had only told him not to bite or hurt people, but they had not forbidden him to hiss—he could hiss, but did not have to bite! They went on their way, and later when the villagers came and tried to pester the snake, he started hissing and everyone ran away and he was left in peace.

This hissing is part of the natural phenomena. Although it seems like an act, it is part of nature and it fits that situation; it was designed by the Absolute that hissing can be performed by the snake, if he is a snake, so that he can save his skin. In the same way in our daily life there are situations when such hissing is necessary as a safeguard, and one should not hesitate to resort to methods which can resolve situations without causing any change or disturbance within oneself.

6

The Drama

Water from the Ganges

I know and understand that the Self is one with the Universal Self and this affects my life. I do not fully experience this in meditation, though I often seem on the brink. What stops me there?

In everyone's life one experiences unity with the Universal Self but one does not know it. During deep sleep the Self merges with the Universal Self. This happens in ignorance but it is a natural phenomenon. If during active life or meditation one does not feel this merging, it is because of a sheath. This sheath is natural, too. The unity which is experienced is the light thrown by the Universal Self on this sheath. If the sheath is transparent and pure, then all is well, but if it is cloudy or dirty, one only gets a glimmer. This is the brink of direct experience. If the water in the Ganges were Universal Self, then water taken from the Ganges and put in a bottle would be the individual Self, although the water is the same. Once you open or break the bottle letting the water flow back into the Ganges you would no longer see any difference, and you would not be able to take that water back, for it would have merged with the Ganges again forever. The only thing which has made it different is the sheath which separates the individual Self from the Universal Self.

THE MAN AT THE CINEMA

The Creator created the universe in all its different aspects and forms. He observes the drama which He has created. All who take part in this play and know its mystery and essence are detached. They play their part and enjoy it. Those who do not know its mystery become identified with their parts and are bound by them. When they lose their identification they too can enjoy playing their part in the grand drama without being bound.

There was a man from the country who visited his city relatives. To entertain him the relatives took him to the cinema. They bought expensive tickets for the back row, but their country cousin was insulted at being put at the back and insisted that they sit at the very front. All went well until suddenly a lion appeared on the screen and looked as if it would jump out at the audience. Our friend took his stick and struck at the lion to defend himself. The screen was broken, the film stopped, and the place thrown into darkness and confusion. At first no one could understand what had happened, then they realized that in the audience was a man who had never been to a cinema before and took the film to be real. The same applies to those ignorant people who regard what goes on in the world as the whole reality and become identified and involved, leading to foolish actions; when the real significance of the grand drama is known, these people can play their part with detachment and enjoyment.

THE PUPPETS AND THE CINEMA

The remembrance of the Universal Self during the day is an increasing comfort. Nowadays everything is more pleasant, and even unpleasant things seem less important than before. However, one feels on a dreamy plateau where, because of the pleasant life, the need to keep going on the path is less sharp. One is not complaining about the increased happiness, but though one feels the greater presence during the day, one's meditation does not seem deep enough and one seems more caught in a dreamy phase. Can the Shankaracharya advise?

One of the fundamental characteristics of life on this earth is the illusion of being the independent doer, of having free will. It is very difficult to maintain that individuals are the doers of anything, for the whole creation is a manifestation of the Absolute who is the real doer. He has made his whole show in such a beautiful pattern which keeps changing from one moment to another as creation continues. The whole thing is going on by virtue of the creative impulse given by the Absolute; He is the independent one, He is the free one, and He is the real doer.

Part of the show is our human nature with its capacities of memory and thinking which, if one takes the load of the past and the future upon oneself, makes the journey hard and treacherous, for the past and the future appear terribly big, and it is very difficult to walk along the path if one carries this load. "If such and such action were taken," we think, "then a particular result could be achieved" or "If I hadn't acted the way I did, I could have saved myself from these effects." One should always keep oneself light-hearted and free from that burden. In fact, the load is on the mind itself, the physical body has nothing to do with it, but because the mind governs the physical body, the physical body also suffers.

One of the best analogies is the shadow play of puppets. There is someone holding the strings and moving them, but they appear to be moving themselves and to be the real doers. The whole of creation is very much like a puppet show, with the strings being held by someone else.

Another example is a cinema show, where the film is being shown on the screen and the people keep on looking at these moving pictures. On the screen you see mountains, buildings, seas, and fights, love scenes and religious scenes. All types of scenes are being enacted on this screen. Some people watching are like the puppets, and they get animated by the scenes.

One should be able to see the things which are happening in the world, but only as a silent observer. See all the pleasures on the screen, but don't get involved and driven off course.

All the exciting things which are shown on the screen do not colour the screen itself—the screen is pure white. It has no colour of its own; it just reflects the colours which are thrown on it.

So we should become like a screen where every part of the activity takes place and is allowed to take place, but we should become pure white and not be stained or dyed with any of the colours of the world. It is not our business to have any ambition or desire to initiate a new line of action.

You mentioned the dream state. There are five states: the enlightened state, the awake state, the dream state, deep sleep, and fifthly the unconscious state. All these five states belong to the mysterious creative art of the Absolute. Each of these states is part of the manifested creation for the pleasure of the Self, and in fact, each state is useful for one purpose or another. There is nothing to choose between one or the other. One doesn't have to choose anything, but stand in the middle and see both sides, the outer and the inner, or stay in the present and watch the passing life, the play of past and future. One has to become the impartial and silent observer of whatever happens, whether it is *samadhi*, waking, dreaming, or sleep. If that is achieved, it is beyond all these states of the world we live in, and in effect everything is truth, consciousness, and bliss, the Absolute. Then even the most humdrum work, such as digging, gives bliss or joy.

We forget that we are the master, we are the Absolute, but by studying true knowledge we come to know it again, just as we come to recognise individuals.

Someone's friend may be asked to act a part in a play, so he puts on different clothes, and head-gear and so much make-up he is unrecognisable. But the moment he speaks, the sound of his voice reveals his identity.

Here, the true knowledge is the sound through which one recognises the true Self manifesting through all these different forms. One has to understand and find out this synthesis—that the being within is also manifesting and taking part outside, and one has to discover the unity, to hate no one, and start working through love. That will bring peace and liberation.

THE DEMON RAKSHU FIGHTING INDRA

Some years ago the Shankaracharya said that we need to learn to enjoy mind, both in stillness, as in meditation, and also in activity. Could he say more about how one enjoys mind in activity?

The basic nature pervades everything, and once you start experiencing it in all things, then you will be able to enjoy it whatever your circumstance. So the main use of the intellect is in seeing, observing, and feeling the all-pervasiveness of that perfect nature—just as when you see a tree, then your mind should be able to convey to you that the basic nature which is in you is also in the tree.

It is another matter that this basic nature makes its appearance in different forms. In a creeper it is tender, in a stone it is hard, in the leaves of a tree it is green. The form may be different but the basic nature is the same. So when your mind sees or appreciates the fact of the all-pervasiveness of nature, then in your everyday life, your normal duties, you will be able to enjoy the circumstances in which you are placed.

Here is a story from the scriptures:

At one time there was a demon known as Rakshu, who was fighting with Indra. At one stage in the fight Indra was distracted, and his sword slipped out of his hand. Being disarmed, he was afraid that Rakshu would kill him. At this point Rakshu stopped, and said, "Don't worry! We are just playing at fighting, and you have been given this job to fight me, so pick up your sword again and then we will go on fighting, you needn't be afraid." When this sort of feeling develops, you will find that, in whatever circumstances you are placed, you will realize that this is all a play, a drama. Then, whether an enemy faces you, or a beloved one, you will behave as you should on that particular occasion, and your mind will not misguide you. You will be correctly guided.

7

Example

THE CHILD ADDICTED TO SWEETS

The Shankaracharya told us that we should keep our treasure in the heart where it can be used as necessary. I would like to ask further what we can do to ensure that the understanding of an important idea is ever present throughout the day colouring our thoughts and actions.

One has to decide what are good thoughts and what are bad thoughts. This is a decision one has to make. Once a decision is made then one ought to stick to the good thoughts and remind oneself of them as often as one can.

After some time they will have a place in the heart and all activities will be coloured by them. Whatever is not good, judged by one's own decisions, should not be toyed with. If these do come up they should never be given any support—just drop them. At those moments one can encourage good thoughts, supporting and sustaining them. Only in this way would it be possible to live up to the good idea.

There was a certain holy man who was visited by an elderly

lady and a small boy who was addicted to eating sweets. She wanted the influence of the holy man to remove this bad habit. When the holy man heard about this he asked the old woman to come back in a fortnight. After a fortnight when the old woman returned, this holy man simply said to the boy that eating sweets was not a very good habit, it would result in some sort of disease later on: "So, my good boy, you should give them up." The old woman said, "If that's all you had to say, you needn't have bothered me to come back after a fortnight." The holy man said he could not have done this the other day because he himself was in the habit of eating sweets and had no authority to ask anyone else to give them up. So he had to give up eating sweets for a full fortnight and control his own desire, because if he did not control it he could have no authority, and even if he had said the same thing to the boy it would have had no effect. In fact just these few words did the trick. So ultimately it is up to the individual.

If by the application of this knowledge, good company, and use of one's reason, one has definitely found some truth somewhere, then the only thing one has to do is to put it into constant practice. One should never indulge in anything which stands opposed to that goodness or there would never be any moral authority for preaching. So whatever one has decided is wrong, one should not entertain it at all, and all that one has decided is good should always be kept in mind and put into practice. By doing this one would see that the effect on the community, or the people around you, would be positive and good would prevail.

The Old Woman and the Moslem Preacher

In the fifth chapter (v. 7–10) of the *Bhagavad-Gita* it says that all sensory experiences of hearing, seeing, touching, smelling, tasting, sleeping, etc., are the works of nature while the Self is free. People use this freedom of the Self to justify their lack of control over their habits. In fact, they are slaves claiming to be free. They will have to look at these habits in their next lives if they do not see them in this life.

There was a Moslem who used to preach a lot but was not very successful. One day he was about to take his morning drink at a place where an old lady came to clean the table. She dusted it first then wiped it with a wet cloth. Dirty streaks were left behind. The preacher asked her to clean it again, and each time she tried to clean it, the dirty marks followed. Then the preacher asked her to clean the dirty cloth first and then come to clean the table. The old lady retorted, "I am doing exactly as you do. You are a dirty and evil man, yet you go on preaching to others. Don't you know that, like me, you will never succeed?" The preacher was astonished to hear the truth; he very humbly paid her respect for the valuable lesson and then started to clean his own being first. Later he was successful and became a famous saint of the Islamic world.

Gandhi and the Spices

There is an interesting incident from the life of Mahatma Gandhi. He had an ashram of his own in Sabarmati where he used to live with some twenty-five of his followers. The discipline was hard and austere. Food was limited to three simple things without spices or chillies. Once a few guests from Marvar (a part of Rajasthan) came to stay. They did not like the simple food and did not eat much the first day. So they bought spices and chillies from the market and used them with the simple food. The cook objected, but next day they again used them. The cook tried to impress upon them that the regulations and discipline of the ashram did not allow such liberties, and they had better refrain from such habits, but they were unable to resist. So the matter was brought to the notice of Mahatma Gandhi. He also instructed them to refrain but to no avail. When they used the spices again, Gandhi summoned them to the meeting and in front of all the people he beat himself on the head. People were surprised at his behaviour and asked why he did such a thing. Gandhi replied, "There must be some such desire hidden in my own nature if my guests can't follow me, so I must get this out of my own system. Only then will my words have some effect on these gentlemen." After that no one ate chillies or spices any more in his ashram.

The Birds Whose Eggs Were Washed Away

In the children's game of seeking the treasure, or hunt the thimble, with the child blindfolded, we say 'hot' or 'cold' to guide him to the treasure. In my search for the Self I would like someone to say 'hot' or 'cold' to guide my steps.

Within each person, there lives the Universal Self along with the individual Self for the purpose of guidance. Therefore,

EXAMPLE   67

we get a guiding voice from time to time when we are in difficulties. In order to hear that inner voice, we should pray to the all-knowing Universal Self in solitude with a settled mind. Then an answer, to bring us face to face with success, is sure to come forth. Therefore, what we have to do is to take inner guidance from that immense source of power, the Universal Self, with fullest concentration of mind and humility. If we were to do so, then the question of hunting for treasure with eyes blindfolded would not arise.

As compared with the huge size of the universe in which we live, this human body of ours is like a speck of dust. Compared with the unlimited consciousness of the Absolute, our mind is like a drop in the ocean. The problem before us is how to tackle that great consciousness with such limited means—a hopeless task apparently! But hope comes from the saying "God helps those who help themselves" which, fortunately, is true.

The real cause of failure is not the inadequacy of the means but an inadequacy of understanding and determination. Provided we understand what is required, and provided our determination to shed the burden we carry is strong enough, a very little can achieve great results, because on seeing the invincibility of our determination, the heart of the Absolute melts and He Himself comes to our aid.

You have said, "But my efforts seem ineffectual. Like digging a very large field—it sometimes seems the spade is not enough—a tractor is required!" After all, the field you speak of is by no means too large for the mind. All fields are smaller than the soul, all lying within the mind, but we feel small in the field of life. If, instead, we remember that we are great, we are infinite, and that all possible fields come from within our own soul and mind, then our mind gives an appropriate decision on each problem immediately. But this is possible only if we do not try to restrict or imprison our mind in this small body.

The Self contains the soul, the soul contains the mind, and the mind contains the body. But ordinarily people think of it the other way round, i.e., that it is the body which contains all that. Here lies the mistake. The moment we take a broad view of our soul and mind, the whole universe goes into it.

The manager of an estate gets on well only by listening to the voice of the proprietor. Similarly, in physical life, it is beneficial to recognise the voice of the Universal Self that lives in the soul. People endowed with higher intelligence recognise the voice of the Universal Self. Ordinary people can get this guidance through prayers and solitude, and this guidance can solve the hardest of problems. The small spade you mention is after all a child of the tractor. If it would call for the help of the tractor, that help would not be denied in view of the relationship between the two. Then the small spade would do the work of the tractor satisfactorily.

A story illustrates how great powers come to the help of the weak as a result of firm determination:

A pair of birds lived by the seashore, and laid their eggs on a high rock. One day huge waves came and washed the eggs away. The birds were very upset at this uncalled-for act of cruelty on the part of the sea, and they made up their minds to fill it up. They took a little sea water in their beaks and dropped it on land, and took a little sand from the land and dropped it into the sea. They did this from morning till evening day after day.

One day a great saint named Agastya appeared and asked the birds how they hoped to fill up the sea with such attempts. The birds replied that, since the sea had swept away their children without any provocation, they would go on trying to fill up

EXAMPLE 69

the sea all their life. Even after death they would wish to be born again and again to continue that work till it was completed. The saint was surprised and impressed with such firm determination on the part of the two tiny birds. As he had supernatural powers he ordered the sea to return the birds' eggs at once and the waves deposited the eggs back on the rock.

This is just a fairy story. Now we shall examine what it represents. The saint was the Absolute. The birds were man. The sea was the world. And man's true and firm aspirations were the eggs. When man (the birds of this story) sets himself on a true and unshakeable purpose, then the Absolute (the saint) gives him full assistance, and problems (the waves of the sea) bow down in submission.

THE TEACHER AND THE RECLUSE

Can a realized man pass on Self-realization only by words or by other means?

There are two types of realized men, the teacher and the recluse. The first is the teacher who practises what he teaches. He comes to people to impart his knowledge and open the way for development of mankind. He talks to them, gives necessary training, looks after them, and keeps on guiding them towards Self-realization.

The other type is the recluse. Although his influence affects the world because of his being, he doesn't like to mix with the masses. He would speak in a way which could confuse ordinary men.

In the teaching tradition the teacher practises for himself and also uses his powers to help others to develop. His presence in the world is not so much for his own attainment but to enable others to have what he has. The recluse does not work in this way. He seeks solitude to enjoy the Self and does not invite any intrusion. When once in a while he appears among the multitude, he intentionally appears ordinary so as not to attract attention. If someone recognised him he might help them due to their sincerity or he might just ignore them. The influence of the recluse creates a good atmosphere.

In olden days in India, a brahmin lived with his four children. One of them was Jadabharat. He wouldn't learn anything nor do any job. His father tried hard but nothing happened. He only meditated.

His family did not understand that, in fact, he was a saintly man. When his father died, his brothers, who were fully educated and married, tried to use him as a guard for the house. The housewives started looking after him a little and would give him left-over food. He didn't complain and happily ate anything that was offered. The brothers got tired of this and removed him from the house. For some time the neighbours looked after him, but there was no improvement. He was asked to protect the crops from animals and birds, but he would cry out only after they had eaten their full share. He proved good for nothing and was kicked out of the village and was captured by a group of people who used to sacrifice human beings. He was cleaned and fully dressed for the ceremonial sacrifice, but before he could be slain the deity appeared, saved his life, and destroyed the killers. From there he went roaming around and was again taken on as a carriage-bearer of a king called Raghugana, who was going to meet a sage called Kapila. Jadabharat didn't move

EXAMPLE 71

steadily but set his feet down here and there, which made the carriage move up and down. The king became so uncomfortable that he came down and taunted him saying that perhaps it was very difficult for him to carry the load because he was thin and weak, knowing that he looked strong and healthy. Jadabharat didn't want to be killed. If the king hit him perhaps that would bring about his destruction. So in order to save himself he said, "I am made of dust, the carriage is made of dust, and he who sits in the carriage is also made of dust. Dust doesn't feel anything and the true Self is not bound by dust, so why should the Self feel uncomfortable?" This opened the eyes of the king and he paid his respects to him. Then Jadabharat left him without another word. He was the recluse type of realized man.

8

Faith

RAMDAS AND THE BOIL

A Christian saint, Augustine, once said, "A man becomes what he loves. If he loves a stone he becomes a stone; if he loves mankind, he becomes a man, and if he loves God, I dare not say more for you might stone me." Can you comment?

According to the Advaita system this would mean if you worship a stone as a stone, you become a stone. But if you worship the stone as the Absolute, then you become the Absolute. There is nothing like a mere stone in this creation. The stone is one form of the same substance which exists everywhere in creation. It is the same force working through men, vegetation, or minerals. All that we see, the stone, the man, and everything, is not real in itself. The reality behind everything is the same *Sat, Chit, Ananda*—Truth, Consciousness, and Bliss. Once you have separated and purified it, and removed the limitation of ignorance, you will be able to see Truth, Consciousness, and Bliss even in the stone.

We have a beautiful story of a saint from South India who

was called Saint Ramdas who had a following of thousands of disciples. One day he decided to test them, so he pretended to be sick due to a boil on his leg. What he did was to take a mango and tie it on to his leg and put a bandage round it so that people would think there was a large swelling. He said, "Well now, I am suffering from this poisonous boil. I do not think I will survive and it seems my end is near. However, there is a possibility that if someone were to suck the poison out of this boil I might be saved, but this unfortunate man would have to die from the poison." They all started looking at one another but no one came forward.

After quite a long time the educated disciples who used to look after the theological and administrative part of his work throughout India assembled and said to the saint, "Swami, since you have drawn near your end and there is no other possibility, would you like to dictate the terms of your will to form a trust, so that the management of these disciples and the teaching may be carried on?" They did not mention anything else. But from among them one person came forward and said, "I am ready to do anything for you in whatever way you please." Then Ramdas told him that he would have to suck the poison but he would die. He replied, "If thousands of people are going to derive wisdom from your survival, then my loss of life will be a great gain to me. I will be happy to give my life for a purpose like this," and before anybody could check him he forced himself on Ramdas and started sucking the poison, but to his great surprise it was a sweet mango. The trick was thus exposed and most of the disciples felt the shame of not rising to the occasion and only pretending to love the saint.

Only very few really love, for true love is something very rare. One can see these two types of love, *prem* (true love) and *moha* (attachment), in simple terms. If you want happiness or pleasure from the beloved, then your love is deluded attachment, but if you sacrifice everything for the pleasure of the beloved, then it is true love.

THE KING'S DAUGHTER AND THE FALSE GURU

Everything is consciousness, and nothing is lifeless, or senseless. An object like a tree can teach you so much that you could find yourself face to face with the Ultimate Reality or God.

A king's daughter was taking a stroll in her garden with her mother. She noticed one flower which was just budding, another which was in full bloom, and yet another which had dried up and fallen. She pointed them out to her mother. The mother said that the three flowers summed up the whole story of life and if she wanted further enlightenment, she should find a guru.

The girl began to search for a good guru for herself. An impostor came to know all this, and posed before her as a very learned guru, so the girl requested him to initiate her into the true knowledge. The impostor asked her to give him all her money, which she did at once, then he took her to a lonely place and tied her to a tree. Then he went away, telling her that he was testing her, and that she was to remain like that till he came back and untied her.

She remained tied up, uncomplaining, for a long time, such was her faith in the guru. The god, Vishnu, was impressed by her devotion. He sent the saint, Narada, to untie her, but she refused, saying that only her guru must untie her. Then Vishnu sent Narada to find the imposter. He was found and brought there. Vishnu ordered him to untie her at once, and the false guru and Vishnu both stood before the girl. Even then the girl wondered whether she should salute the guru first, or Vishnu, because it was the guru who had been instrumental in bringing Vishnu to her. Thus, even a false guru can provide us with enlightenment, provided the disciple is fully devoted to him.

The guidance of holy men can always help us out of our difficulties.

SHIVA HOLDING THE POISON

When I came in here this morning, I felt complete reassurance of the absolute unity that exists in all things, and I was again completely certain that there is no need for any anxiety, and that all things are cared for. How can one hold that?

When one comes to certain places which exercise a particular type of influence, just as you describe, there are two ways of holding this experience. One is by the mind, by thought or intellect. If it is held by the mind constantly and one reminds oneself about the experience and the taste of the experience, or the content of the experience, then in the course of time it becomes one's own.

The second way of holding the experience is to hold it by faith and that is held in the emotional body. It is held very tight; this is where it is held totally. Having held the experience from these two standpoints, from faith and from mind or thought, then it becomes one's own. Then whenever, or under whatever circumstances, or under whatever influences one may be, one will never lose this experience, and one will be able to share these influences wherever one goes.

There is an example from the life of a mahatma. He used to say that all movement was poisonous—not useful to the Self—and yet there was movement all over the creation. So it has to be held somewhere, otherwise the bliss of the ocean would not be experienced and the Self would not manifest.

In Indian mythology Shiva is depicted as holding poison in his throat. He does not allow it to go to either the outside or the inside body, or it would kill the truth about both the outer and the inner world. So he simply holds it at the threshold of the outer and inner body. He can do this because he is always in *samadhi*.

Anyone who has acquired the taste of this great unity of peace in which everybody's soul is cared for, feels that if he could hold this he would, like Shiva or Shankara, be able to keep the peace himself and provide it for others who need it. Thus Shankara is one who has the peace and can bring peace to everyone.

The Devotee Who Milked a Lioness

It seems that it is bad thoughts about situations or people that chiefly separate me from the Absolute. Are good actions—ordinary duties done with attention, even dedication—more powerful than trying to keep bad thoughts away?

We often do not realize the powers which we can command or acquire through purity of purpose. Knifing a human body is a serious crime in the ordinary way, yet surgeons do it daily because of the purity of their purpose. Similarly, soldiers even kill human beings on the battlefield without becoming legally guilty of murder.

Once I went to a circus and there I saw a lion on the stage with a goat standing on its head. The attention of the lion was not on the goat in any way because its attention was on the gun which the tamer held right in front of its eyes.

There are two motives for performing good deeds. One is where human beings are terrified of the Absolute, as the lion was terrified of the weapon, knowing for certain that if they do anything wrong they will be punished instantly, and they will have to suffer. If they are so terrified of the Absolute's power they will not do anything wrong. The other way is to have so much love for the Absolute that no bad thoughts will visit them at all because there will be no scope for a bad thought. Every part of their being will be permeated by the Absolute, leaving no room for anything bad.

There is an example from the life of the saint, Ramdas. He had a Maratha king as disciple—Shiva Ji. Once the saint had a pain in his stomach and although a number of physicians tried, they could not cure it. All his disciples were worried as to what could be done for this ailment. The saint said it would not be cured by ordinary medicine, all he needed was a little milk from a lioness. If someone could bring that, he would rub the milk on his navel and that would cure the pain. This was a test for them! As you know it is very difficult to get the milk of a lioness, but this brave king, Shiva Ji, took it upon himself to go into the jungle and look for a lioness. He took a small vessel with a little cloth inside. Flies gathered round the den of a lioness and these led him to it; he went in and saw a lioness with two cubs lying on the ground. When he entered the cave, the smell of the man alerted her, and she sprang to her feet and started growling.

Then Shiva prayed and said he had come as a friend, not as an enemy and meant no violence at all; all he was interested in was getting a few drops of milk to cure his teacher. Would she offer some? At this point the lioness lay down again and he squeezed out a few drops of milk, came back to the saint, offered them to him, and the saint was cured. People were astonished and asked how Shiva managed to get the milk, and he told them the story.

If one has complete faith in and complete love for the Absolute then every situation is a friendly situation and will turn into something good however dangerous or violent it seems on the ordinary level.

In order to escape from bad thoughts or bad actions these are the only two possible ways—either one is possessed by fear of the Lord, or one is possessed by love of the Lord.

9

Ignorance

THE MONGOOSE AND THE SNAKE

If, during the working day one suffers from plain forgetfulness, can the Shankaracharya recommend any technique or method whereby the aspirant can keep the teaching in mind throughout the day?

During the working day one is involved in activity. Because of the nature of activity, one thing you have to be forgiven is that you forget your longing for the divine; it is a natural phenomenon. But, if it is natural to forget, it is also natural to remember. So, when one knows that one has forgotten, one should remind oneself of what one has forgotten, and try to place this forgetful state between two moments of remembrance.

If the darkness, which symbolises forgetfulness, is contained between two lights then it is very easy to cross the darkness without any help from outside, because there is light behind and light in front.

So remembering does reflect some light and one can hold on to the light that lies ahead and pass through the darkness.

If there are two moments of remembering, then one can see

that the forgetfulness in between them loses its force and, whatever is needed by the individual will be made available by remembering again.

There is a small creature called a mongoose whose nature is to fight snakes. Whenever they meet they fight, and when the poison of the snake enters the body of the mongoose through a bite, the mongoose runs away from the fight and goes to smell a certain type of herb. By smelling this particular herb the poison of the snake is neutralised and the mongoose is restored to health. He then returns to the fight, and this process can go on as long as the fight continues.

Forgetting is very much like this poison from the snake, which activity causes in our nature. One need not bother about it, one simply needs to go and get the help of the herb. By remembering the teaching all this will be easy, and forgetting will have no bad effects.

We should handle our faithful servant, the ordinary moving mind, very gently and encourage it daily to make progress, using methods of love and holy ideas. In spite of being a mere servant, its powers are great, though it is very small compared to the Self. If we use force or fear to reform it we cannot attain the same success as we would achieve by love and holy thoughts. We should all the time keep on reminding this servant of the fact that the Self is eternal, whereas sensory pleasures are only momentary.

Of course, difficulties do arise in the course of changing the addiction of the mind from bad to good company, but ultimately we can win. We should never allow ourselves to feel helpless; we should always be the master of our own house. In the *Bhagavad-Gita*, chapter 2, verse 3, Krishna urges Arjuna to shed petty weaknesses of the heart and get ready for the impending battle.

Thus, we should always see ourselves in our full stature, which is very great. The servant really can be trained to give up its old habits, just as a civilised person would not put bad food into his mouth.

You remember the story of the fight between the mongoose and the snake? When the snake bites the mongoose, the latter runs away to smell the herb which neutralises the poison, and then comes back to fight so that, finally, it is always the snake that is killed.

In the present context sensory pleasures are the poison and awakened thinking the medicine, and it is the true Self that wins the battle.

The Holy Man Who Tried to Stay at the Palace

The Creator has provided everything one needs. Why is it that there is a barrier to remembering this?

The Self is a part of the Absolute. The Absolute is the source of all creation. The Self is surrounded by creation, and amid the multiplicity and diversity of creation it is ignorant of the unity and reality. The Absolute is limitless, creative, the giver, never claiming anything, for "He is." The Self is separated from the Creator only by ignorance. This is why we have limits or boundaries. We possess and we claim; this is all ignorance. The Absolute created the universe and we create boundaries—"This is my land, this is my country." In fact the land belongs to no one. You can claim it for a time, but in the end you have to leave everything behind. The Creator creates men; we create the 'Indian' and the 'English.' The creation is consciousness, but we do not see this because of our ignorance.

Once a holy man was travelling. In the evening he asked to stay the night at a palace. He asked the doorkeeper, who enquired of the owner. The owner refused and said that this was not an inn where people could drop in.

The holy man asked the owner, "Who built this palace?"

"My father," came the answer.

"Now you own the palace?"

"Yes, I am the owner."

"Who will own it after you?"

"My sons," said the owner.

"Who after your sons?"

"My grandsons."

"Then this looks like an inn," said the holy man, "because people seem to come and stay for some time and go. Wouldn't you call it an inn? Had it belonged to your father, he certainly could have taken it with him."

The owner realized his error. As long as the Self is obscured by this ignorance, as long as it claims ownership, it will not remember, it will not unite with the Absolute. When one knows the truth, one breaks down the barrier and unites with the Absolute.

One always has the tendency to think of what I want from the holy man. If only one could see with the eye of the holy man what one should want, it would be more appropriate.

An individual is working for Self-realization. The realized man looks at it differently. He knows that there is no such thing as Self-realization. The Self is itself real, who can make it more real? What one is really doing is trying to remove the cloud of ignorance. The eye can see perfectly well by sunlight. If there is a cloud the vision may become dim; the thicker the cloud, the dimmer the vision. The eye is like the Self, the sun is like the Absolute and the cloud is ignorance. This is the barrier. The eye and the sun are made of the same element. The more light there is, the more the darkness disperses. The moon gives more light than lamps, the sun gives more light than the moon. Two suns will give more light than one and so on. When one gets the light of the Self, which is the Absolute, then even the suns become brighter. That is when unity is seen. Unity is there; the Self, which is real, is there. It is only a matter of enlightenment. This is how it seems to a realized man.

DATTATRAYA AND HIS TWENTY-FOUR TEACHERS

Could we hear more about the outer influences which help to unify the subtle body?

The subtle body consists of mind, intelligence, memory, and ego, and realization of the subtle body means doing away with the ignorance surrounding it. If one is attentive one can see many things happening outside oneself. Although there are two worlds, within and without, the one within can fortify itself with good ideas, good thinking, and good resolutions. These will help one's subtle body to clear away ignorance.

As far as the outer world is concerned we are surrounded by good influences, but these influences can be gathered only if one is attentive and recognises them. Here books, good company, holy men, grace, and even ordinary events can be helpful.

Shri Dattatraya (chapter 11 of the *Shrimad Bhagavatam*) had twenty-four teachers in his life. This means he gathered teaching useful for the growth of his subtle body from twenty-four different incidents in his life, even from birds and elephants. There is also a story about a girl, as follows:

Once, while he was going round the town, he came to a house where all the men had gone out to work and there was only a young girl at home who was about to be married. Parents from another town had come to see if she was a suitable bride for their son. There was no one else to entertain the guests so she had to do everything herself. She was very poor and had not much to offer them. She thought she would prepare some rice for them, but even the rice was not ready, and she had to remove the husks before cooking it. While she was trying to do this by beating the rice with a wooden hammer her bangles made a noise, and she thought her guests would hear the noise and realize the household did not even have rice. She wanted to save the honour of the house, so she started to break some of the bangles, but she found when even two remained there was still some noise, so she broke them all except one.

Dattatraya observed all this. She also invited him to wait for some rice, and he stayed. After eating he said that when one has to meet one's most respected guest one has to keep all disturbance away, and the disturbance can only be removed after the world of disturbances is broken off.

So, in meditation one goes to meet the Self which is the greatest of all guests. One has to leave behind all those ideas, thoughts, and worries, and attend to one thing only in order to meet the guest. One can gather and study so many influences

which abound in the universe. It is only a question of being attentive and learning from ordinary things as well as from the
teacher, and accomplishing full dispersion of ignorance from the
subtle body.

THE MOTHER WHO WOULD NOT BLESS HER SON

There was a lord or baron who kept a private army. He was very
ambitious and always liked to cross his own boundaries and sub-
due other lands. His people supported him and were very loyal,
so it was always quite a pleasant adventure for him. Each time
he returned to his own castle all his people honoured him and
praised him and the glory of his victories. When he had heard
all this he would go to his mother and ask for her blessing. His
mother was not pleased, so she never gave him a blessing.

After a few such occasions, he plucked up the courage to ask
her why she was displeased. She said, "My dear son, you are
going the wrong way. I would have been very happy if you had
overcome your real enemies which are within you. In fact, because of these glorious victories you have been turning your
back on them and making your enemies within even stronger.
In fact, you are losing the battle every day. If you tried to overcome your greed, your lust, your futile ambitions, and your desire to be a great lord, then I would say you had done a good job
and deserved a blessing."

In all these games which go on in the world like a casino,
the loser certainly loses, but those who win are also the losers
because, in fact, they are gaining nothing.

In the *Isha Upanishad* it says:

Those who say "I know" do not really know the Self. Those who say "I do not know," there is no question of their knowing, they certainly do not know the Self. The real one is neither of these. He never says "I do not know," or "I know," but he acts as the Self because he is the Self. One can gain wealth and feel fortunate, but the fortune is misery. Meditation does away with all physical wealth whatever it may be.

INDRA AND BRAHMA

In pursuit of spiritual development, people usually meet two types of leader. The first type belong to the yogic system. They have gone through the eightfold system and through that arduous discipline they have achieved certain powers which they can use for their disciples or even for their own ends. They can show certain miraculous powers. Their disciples love them and have faith in them, and as long as the miracles work their disciples continue to follow them. Later, however, either the disciples break away, or genuinely take to the true discipline themselves and work out their own liberation, or achieve some miraculous powers for their own use and satisfaction. There they stop.

The other type is the wise or holy man who does not care for external or physical miracles and teaches through knowledge, being, meditation, or devotion. He works on the removal of his disciple's impurities, distractions, and attachments, knowing that the Self does not need any development, for it is the

Absolute itself. Only ignorance in the form of impurities, distraction and attachments surround the disciple, so that the real Self cannot exercise its truth, consciousness, and bliss. To achieve the removal of these causes of ignorance, the teacher prescribes certain disciplines for the conduct of life, gives his followers knowledge by which they can arouse reason and correct their mistakes themselves, and he also arouses emotion to lead them to devote their energies to the Universal Self. He has to keep the momentum going continuously, and often applies a little fire to make the disciple stronger.

Just as a potter makes different objects from wet clay and then fires them to make them dry and firm, and only then can these objects be useful; similarly heat must be applied to disciples so that they have more strength to persevere towards truth and not break under temptation.

This work goes on till the disciple himself feels that he has arrived or he is free and he now knows. Once a disciple came to ask if I could say that he now knew. One could only laugh at such a situation for it is like looking for the sun with the light of a lamp. How can anyone else judge the Self? If someone knows, then he never asks anyone else's approval. Self-realization can't be proved by certificates, recommendations, or affirmations by anyone. When the Self knows itself to be free, only then is it free. If anyone pretends to be free then he is only deceiving himself.

Indra and Virochana went to Brahma for the teaching. Brahma told them, "This body is the Absolute, go and realize this." Virochana was satisfied and he worked to make his body beautiful and enjoy it. Indra found that the body was subject to growth, decay, and destruction, so it could not be the Absolute and he came back for clarification.

He was asked to follow the discipline for thirty years before a further lesson could be given. After thirty years he was told that "senses are the Absolute," at which he again protested. After another period of discipline he was told that mind and intelligence were the Absolute. Indra said that they sometimes acted rightly, sometimes wrongly, so they could not be the Absolute, for the Absolute cannot be subject to any change. Another long period of discipline was imposed and then he was told that the conscious body of knowledge was the Absolute. When by his own reasoning he found out that this also was not true, then he was asked to stay for yet another eleven years. At the end of all these years he came to realize that the Self alone is the Absolute, for only the Self knows all things through all the body, senses, etc.

There can never be a moment when one does not know the Self. The Self is the master, the Absolute, the authority. When the Self says, "I know," then it knows.

Self-realization is by the Self. The test of all work and use of all discipline and knowledge and devotion is only this, and when the disciple comes to the point where he sees himself in the light of truth, then he knows that he knows. Then there is nothing more to ask, nothing left to achieve.

THE SCHOOLBOY AND THE PENKNIFE

Vyasa (the author of the *Mahabharata*) says, "I have made a critical study of the Vedas and the scriptures several times. The gist of all that, as I found, is that we should think of the Universal Self all the time." As soon as any thought enters the mind, we are in the grip of ignorance or the illusion of separateness, which catches hold of us and takes us very, very far away.

The individual Self is part of the Universal Self, and it has come into the world for the sake of discovering joy. But, instead of that, it has fallen into the trap of ignorance. Ignorance is forgetting reality. It is the root cause of all the troubles associated with the world. Therefore the greatest of all the troubles is to forget reality, and by that we mean forgetting that only God or Universal Self is real and the sensory world is unreal.

A schoolboy was given a new penknife by his parents for his birthday, and took it to school with him. Usually he carried it in his bag, but that day he put the new one in his pocket. When he wanted it he forgot that it was in his pocket and searched for it again and again in his bag. Not finding it, he thought his classmates had stolen it, and reported the theft to his teacher. The whole class was punished. This is how a most ordinary instance of forgetting causes big trouble.

All worldly objects are like children's toys—a toy elephant, a toy motor car, a toy locomotive, etc. They must be treated as nothing more than toys. Disappointments and trouble will be our lot if we treat them as reality. Therefore, all troubles which we encounter in our life are due to treating the world as real.

What are the best ways of remembering the Universal? How do we establish this connection?

The connection is there already, you don't have to establish it. But what happens is that when we get involved in worldly affairs the power or energy which we get is diminished. However, when we remember our connection with the Universal we feel joy, we feel happy about it. You need to take medicine when you fall ill, so you need to remember your connection with the Universal when you forget it. If you do not forget it, there is no need to remember, the remembrance will be there automatically. Now every time you feel you have forgotten, you have to remember to establish your connection—that is the easy way, because the connection is there, although forgotten. You have only to remember it.

10

Illusion

LAKSHMAN'S DIVE

What is the relation between our sense of time and our state of consciousness? When we go to sleep at night, we lose all sense of time; in our ordinary daytime state, there is no time for what we want to do; in moments of consciousness there seems to be plenty of time; in bliss, or happiness, again time ceases.

Is it true that the time of events on the subtle level is very rapid compared with that on the level of the body? One can seem far away from the Self one minute and then everything can change instantaneously. People seem to be pessimistic and hopeless when they think of Self-realization in slow physical time.

All events take place only at the physical level, though their effects pass on to higher levels also. But the intervals of time and space decrease with rising levels. A thing which appears far off at the physical level, such as Self-realization, is not so at the subtle level.

There are different categories of time. One day we think we
have very little time, but actually there is enough. Another day
we think we have plenty of time, but really it is very short. Time
mostly relates to the situation. In sleep we experience a lot, we
seem to cover a long period of time, but as a matter of fact a long
dream takes only moments to pass through our consciousness.
There is a difference between the sense of time in dreams and
in our waking state. Time is different again in deep sleep, and
in bliss as well. So time varies according to the situation.

Here is an illustration from the *Ramayana:*

Lakshman, the brother of Rama, told him that he would like
to see the great illusion of *Maya* (the drama of creation) which
Rama was always talking about. Rama replied, "You will get into
trouble through seeing it, so I shouldn't bother about it." Lakshman replied, "I'm quite sure it won't affect me, and I'm still curious to see it." So Rama said, "All right, you'll see it by and by,"
and left the question open. They went to the river to bathe.

When they had finished bathing and both were coming
ashore, Rama said, "My brother, I've lost my ring, do you think
you could dive for it?" Lakshman went and dived for the ring;
at that moment he lost consciousness. When he came out of
the water, he was in a different land, in lovely countryside.
There he met a beautiful woman, and they settled down
together, established a home and lived like householders. He
had four sons, and when he became an old man he caught
malarial fever, developed a cough, and eventually died. His
sons took him to the river. The custom was to immerse the
body in the water. At the moment the body was submerged
Lakshman came out of the world of illusion and found himself back on the river bank.

He went to Rama with tears in his eyes and repentance in

his heart, but still did not remember what had happened. Rama said to him, "You wanted to experience the world of illusion. Now you have experienced it."

All the differentiation of time and space which we calculate in this world, is the illusion. In the Self or in Brahman (the Absolute) there is no time, there is no space. It is all one. We see a distorted effect of all this in our worldly consciousness or sleep. The differentiation of time is illusion, for it is, as I said at the beginning, always different.

In the story of Lakshman and the ring, in what sense was it that both the views of the world as seen by Lakshman when under the water and by Rama were illusory?

The story tells of two states, one like a dream world in sleep, and the other the world we ordinarily see when awake. The world of dreams has no independent existence, only the memory of one's experience in the common waking state. The dreams would appear according to one's attachment to certain types of experience. When 'awake' the dream world is known as illusion. For the benefit of people under discipline this example of one world and of two states of our own experience is described in the story, so that they may understand the validity of the third state (which knows both of these as illusion). Taken rightly, the other two states should be regarded just as an actor regards his role in a play (now on-stage, then off-stage).

This story has made a deep impression on some people who felt that if they could really understand it, they would be clear about many important things. Are not these states being experienced simultaneously? After all, we have the Universal Self within us experiencing the conscious view of the world while I, ego, is experiencing the illusion.

There are two types of people—the knowers and those who don't know. In the case of the knowers, all their activities conform to their inner state and the way they understand the world. For them there is no attachment, and for such a man, life is just a drama or play, so he is free and happy. The ones who don't know keep looking at the result of their activities, or actions, and because of this they get bound to chains of desire, activity, and result.

So many diseases can overtake someone in such a state and this results in poor growth and a poor state of health of the physical body which causes, of necessity, both a closing of the mind as well as cramp and tension of body and muscles. In due course this leads to illness of mind as well as body.

This truth about life being a drama or play causes great antagonism in Western people. They believe so intensely in their own ideas about the motives of their actions and the results they expect to get from them, that they feel they can't carry on unless they 'believe in what they are doing.'

Not only in the West! This is a common problem. Here in India also there are some people enjoying great so-called 'success' in life; they have a well-ordered household, and do a very efficient day's work in a well paid job. But only when they catch a glimpse of their peaceful Self, or when they see the peaceful Self in other people, only then do they realize the importance of the peace and the Self, and their inner nature compels them to look for it. Some make efforts and even if those are not obviously successful, they at least cherish the idea. This factor alone gives a ray of hope that they will turn to the simple and fundamental idea of treating the world as a play and yet be effective and happy.

KRISHNA AND RADHA

When Krishna met his beloved Radha he told her she looked like the moon. Radha felt humiliated and walked away in distress. Then Krishna felt very lonely and started looking for Radha everywhere and asked all his milkmaids to pacify Radha and bring her back. Radha came back disguised as Krishna and they both tried to establish their right to Radha. They then agreed to go to the milkmaids for identification. The milkmaids were so in love with Krishna that anybody they saw looked like Krishna, and this multiplied the confusion. In this confusion Krishna guessed that the other Krishna was none other than Radha and drew her close and kissed her; thus unity was once more established.

This story has a subtle meaning. When Krishna relates his Self, Radha, to the moon, duality is established. In search of unity he wanders here and there. Even though he has with him the Kingdom, Radha in disguise, he refers to his many I's (the milkmaids) for identification, and confusion is the result. It is only when Krishna recognises the real Radha the illusion disappears and unity is once again established.

THE HORSE AND THE NOISY WELL

This drama-making or illusion of creation keeps entering and confusing the inner world, and comes between oneself and the real Self, and between oneself and one's teacher. How can we take things simply and sincerely?

As long as one knows that there is an agency to create confusion between the two, the effect of this agency is very slight. The real confusion is when you take it as real, and don't see it as an obstacle, then it has power. If you understand that illusion comes in between you and the Self or between disciples and their teacher, then the effect will be very slight. You know the obstacles are there, but they are not deadly because they don't have any hold on you. So this knowledge of confusion and some agency coming in between is helpful.

Is this what prevents one from being a quiet recording machine which does not pick up all background noises too?

The drama of creation is a universal act and this has to go on for all eternity. It will never stop. So all these obstacles and the confusion and everything else will always be there. As long as you don't play and get involved with them, if you are not interested in them you can avoid them, just as right now you took no notice of the mobile loudspeaker which went down the road. So it is good to avoid them simply and sincerely. Violent obstacles must be handled carefully, for they can be very explosive, so extra effort should be made to avoid them. But the ordinary obstacles and confusions are a part of the creation and part of our lives; we cannot undo them and if someone wanted a completely quiet place, devoid of any distraction, it would be hard to find one. The remedy is just to ignore the lot and pick up what is important. One has to use discrimination. For example:

There was a king who rode out on a horse and after some time both he and his horse became very thirsty. In his search for water, he came across a well from which water was being pumped up by mechanical means. The pump made a lot of noise and his horse would not drink because it was nervous and distracted by the noise. So the king asked the workman to stop it for a little while so his horse could drink. But when they stopped the pump, of course, there was no water available. He tried two or three times, and then the foreman of the gang said, "Dear King, if you can make your horse drink this water in spite of the noise, well and good; otherwise look for somewhere else instead!"

The moral is that our moving mind is like the horse. Although it is interested in drinking the water of spiritual knowledge, it is so lost in the distraction of outward noise that it cannot drink. Wise men, however, while aware of these noises, ignore them, and pay attention only to what is useful to the Self.

HANUMAN'S SERVICE TO RAMA

How can the daily activities of a job in life be brought more under good influences? There are rare and wonderful times when a feeling of only being the instrument in trying to help people is felt. How can we make these moments more frequent?

Suppose one is engaged in caring for infants or small children: then there is never a sense of duty, work, service, obligation, help, sacrifice or any other form of ego, for it is only play. This play is due to love, which is like an ocean in which two bodies are engaged in a certain type of movement. There is nothing besides love; no idea of personality or ego arises from either side.

This is real work. Here people are only instruments and the creation is bliss. If one could establish the same relationship in daily work, then the doer would be an instrument and the receiver would also be an instrument, and the two would become One. The unity thus achieved would become a fountain of happiness. We all experience such moments of joy when we remove our layers of individuality or personality or any type of ego. The remedy is simple. Give up all idea of being the doer and it will all be bliss everywhere.

Hanuman (the monkey god) is an example. He only knew service and never knew he was serving, never looked for any results. To him the pleasure of his master was all he cared for. He never meditated, never went into *samadhi*, never engaged himself in study of the scriptures or spiritual discussions. His only service was what he could do with his whole attention. When his lord the Rama of Ayodhya was being enthroned with his wife Sita, then all the servants were being given some reward for their services. Having given rewards to all the others, Rama asked Sita to give a reward to Hanuman. Sita gave him her most valuable pearl necklace. He looked at each pearl carefully and then one by one he started to break the pearls and look into them again and again, and finally threw the pieces away.

People at the coronation were amazed at his behaviour and asked him what he was doing. He said that he was looking for his lord's name but since he did not find it, he threw the pearls away for they were useless. They asked, "But you don't find the name of your lord in everything you come across! Can you say that you have his name in your own body?" He tore open his chest and there was his lord sitting within it. Rama then asked Sita to give him only some blessings which would be enough for him. She gave him secret knowledge of the Absolute and manifested nature, with which he was liberated.

The idea is to serve without the idea of any return, not even the idea of bliss.

THE ELEPHANT AND THE MAHOUT

With the idea of enjoying the whole creation with an impartial attitude, one might ask what is good and bad? The question never gets resolved. In fact, there is neither good nor bad; it is simply our labelling. It is our preference for one or the other which makes one good and the other bad.

If one could keep to this state of being the silent impartial observer, one would see that none of these things exists. One stays in the present, and one acts as the occasion demands, and the whole thing passes. Wise men once discussed this question of deriving happiness from all the multifarious aspects of the world, and the discussion led to the conclusion that one should not entangle oneself with either side, physical or subtle, but should simply observe. Because the Absolute is in everything, and this creation is a most efficient mechanical organism which is functioning according to the laws of the Absolute, one should always see the Absolute behind all these passing phases.

One of the listeners at this discussion went away and on the road saw an elephant coming along. He remembered that the Absolute was in everything, so he thought, "The Absolute is in the elephant, so surely it won't harm me." The mahout on the elephant's back kept shouting at him to get out of the way, but the man on the road took no notice until the elephant picked him up and threw him on one side. Then he went back to the wise man to say he had been misinformed: he thought the elephant was the Absolute, and he was the Absolute and the Absolute would not harm the Absolute in any way, but he had!

Then he was told, "You forgot that the mahout was also the Absolute. Because you did not obey the Absolute when he shouted to you, you were punished. You, in fact, selected one of the two. Do not select, do not show prejudice, do not have impertinent preferences, then everything will be clear and you will easily find your way without any hindrance."

THE SWAMI AND THE PUFF ADDER

Once Swami Ramtirtha, who was from the Punjab, saw a black adder in his path; it was a puff adder with its hood open. Ramtirtha just smiled and laughed and said, "Oh my God, You have come before me in such a frightening shape—but forgive me, I don't like Your shape this time, so please go away." And the puff adder went away.

This shows how to behave as an unprejudiced and silent observer who has no duality—no mental division into good and evil.

11

Love and True Knowledge

THE TEMPLE WITH FOUR GATES

How can we connect ourselves to the fountain of knowledge?

There is a fountain of knowledge, and there is a shower of knowledge. The shower is the outside source, the worldly source from books, schools, or holy men. The people who are deeply involved in the material world of pleasure are like pots turned upside down. However heavy the shower, nothing will go into the pot. Such people deprive themselves, shut themselves off and live on a few drops which enter them without their knowledge. Those who keep themselves open usually find plenty to fill their life with peace, bliss, and knowledge. The other type, who seem to be connected to the fountain of knowledge or who have become the fountain of knowledge are rare; they have been on the 'Way' in their previous life and died before realization, such as yogis. It is that accumulated knowledge which forms the fountain in this life. They don't need much from outside. Once the lid is open the fountain springs out.

To reach the fountain ordinary people simply need to open

their pots and allow them to be filled. Only after Self-realization could one reach the fountain of knowledge. The deserving will certainly inherit the fountain. Geography makes no difference. People around the fountain may not be aware of it, whereas someone from a distant land might acquire it simply by his sincerity and devotion. Although everyone will get some influence from the fountain, only one who prepares himself will inherit it.

There was a temple of Sharada, the goddess of wisdom, in Kashmir, where there were four gates: one for virtue, one for wealth, one for desires, and the last one for liberation. The first three were open, but the fourth was closed. Only a realized man could open it. The first Shankaracharya happened to go there and entered the temple through the fourth gate. The learned men of the temple enquired as to how he could open that gate? The goddess Sharada replied that Shankara was a realized man who had reached the fountain.

THE DESTRUCTION OF THE SANDALWOOD TREES

A rich landowner was pleased with one of his employees, a gardener by profession. Wishing to reward him for his faithful service he gave him one of his gardens to tend and use for his own profit. This garden happened to contain some sandalwood, the most valuable wood in India. The gardener, being ignorant of its value, started to cut down the sandalwood trees one by one, burn them up, and sell the charcoal in the ordinary market. By and by the merchant paid him a visit to see how he was getting on. To his horror he saw what he was doing and shouted at him,

"My good man, do you realize that if you took one small piece of one of those sandalwood trees and polished it up, it would fetch a far higher price than all the charcoal made from burning all the trees!" So you must protect true knowledge.

THE GOLDEN GANESH AND THE MOUSE

In the early stages when people have to be taught to appreciate unity, it is always necessary to show the illusion of two before one can be taught that the two are one. Although one is asked to love the truth, or love the Self, or know the Self, or know the truth, in fact there is no duality. There is no lover of the truth, and there is no truth which can be loved by anybody. They are one and the same thing, but for training purposes these words are used.

Take an example from the *Brihadaranyaka Upanishad* which says there is only one and no second. Although it seems as if the one can have two different forms, we have got to learn to go beyond that to realize the oneness of the Absolute.

To see it on a physical level let us take the example of the ocean. When it is still it is taken as one ocean, but when it has waves then one speaks of waves as if they were different from the ocean. Could one separate them? In fact it is not possible. So the truth is the same. The Self knows the Universal Self; there is no other means of knowing because they are one. However, as long as ignorance is there, the illusion of duality will exist. Thus we see Self as something to be known; in fact only the Self can know itself.

Somebody wanted to worship Ganesh, the son of Shiva,

who rides a mouse. He had some gold, so he wanted to make a golden image. He made a big mouse, taking more than half the gold, and a small Ganesh to sit on it. After some time he got into financial difficulties, so he consoled himself with the thought that after all, devotion need not be golden. He could make do with a stone carving or a wood carving.

When he had made up his mind he took his golden deity to sell for cash to relieve his financial difficulties. He took the mouse and Ganesh the god to a jeweller who put each of them on the scale and, according to the weight, offered to pay a hundred rupees for Ganesh and a hundred and fifty for the mouse. This greatly upset the man, who said to the jeweller that surely the god must be worth more than the mouse. The jeweller replied that however the man might value the two things, his only touchstone was the amount of gold; he was a jeweller and the weight was all he was interested in.

The same applies to the love of truth or knowledge. As long as one does not experience the truth this illusion of duality will be there. We have to use this duality to rise above it. Once you have found the unity there is no lover to be loved, it is just the same—no knower to know the truth because it is truth itself.

THE BRAHMIN WHO WANTED A SON IN HIS OLD AGE

There are two types of knowledge, one about how to live in this world and the other about how to prepare the way for the next journey. Here is an illustration from the myths.

There was a brahmin who had a wife, but she could not produce a son. He became obsessed with desire for a son, and when he was already sixty it happened that a holy man passed by. The brahmin begged him to bless him so that he could have a son. The holy man said, "Well, you've already reached old age; what are you going to do with a son? Far better for you now to devote yourself to the spiritual world and prepare yourself for your next journey. You might live to regret having a son." But the brahmin was so infatuated with the idea that he kept pressing the holy man to bless him, saying, "If you are not going to bless me so that I may have a son, I will commit suicide."

The holy man yielded to pressure and promised to do as the brahmin asked. He blessed some fruit, saying, "Give this to your wife to eat and you will have a son." The wife did not want a son, so she gave this fruit to their cow, and instead she adopted a baby which someone in their family had just had, and they cared for him and brought him up.

However, he grew up to be very violent and destructive, and used to beat them up and finally drove them out of the house. They had no place to go, so they retired into the jungle, where they could at least pray to God at the end of their lives. They were very sorry that they had not listened to the holy man.

The cow, who had been given the fruit which had been blessed, gave birth to a man with ears like a cow's; his name was Gopal, which means 'cow-eared man.' He was a holy being (because he was blessed by the holy man), and devoted himself to spiritual studies and activities. After realizing himself, he started looking for the parents for whom he was destined. And when he came through the jungle to the place where these two people were praying and living in seclusion, he stayed there and gave them true knowledge.

This illustration shows that although it may be very attractive to show people miraculous things to satisfy their obsessions, yet this is not the right way. The best way is to have true knowledge.

THE FRUIT OF THE PUMPKIN AND THE MANGO

There are two types of people: those who work predominantly with the head and those who work predominantly with the heart. Those who work with the head are usually prone to too much discussion, and those who work with the heart accept the discipline or the discourse without any reasoning and like to get on with the work. But neither of them is really complete, because the rational man, that is, the one who simply keeps on discussing and does not practise the discipline, would not attain any further state, so he would not be able to reason better or more deeply.

The person who takes the discipline simply on trust, if he faces a person of the other type would not be able to match up to him. Then he would have some inward doubt in his own heart about the discipline and it is quite possible that under the stress of opposing ideas he might give up. Here is a story to illustrate this:

Two people were going to bathe in the Ganges and while they were walking towards the river the man who worked with the head said to the other, "Look at this Creator—he must be a fool because he does not know what he is doing." While they were going along they passed two types of plants: one was a pumpkin growing in the sandy soil above the river with many big pumpkins and six feet away was a mango tree. So the intellectual said, "This is such a small plant and the Creator has put such big fruit on it, and if you look at the mango tree, which is such a big tree, it has such small fruit. So he must be stupid to have done such a thing."

The other man was unable to reply and couldn't say that he knew the Absolute was not so foolish in doing this, so he kept quiet and felt sorry for himself.

When they were returning after their bathe, on their way home they felt tired and thought they would have a little rest beneath a tree. While they were dozing one of the ripe mangoes fell on the nose of the intellectual. It hit him hard and he felt a great deal of pain, but at this moment he exclaimed to the other man that now he understood why the Absolute made such small fruit on big trees. "If he had acted according to me, I would have been wiped out!"

The moral is that both ways are insufficient. The real way is to bring these two together; with both in unison life is better and more purposeful.

RAMAKRISHNA AND VIVEKANANDA

Everyone is capable of having his heart melted, but because of certain circumstances hardening has taken place.

Vivekananda (whose earlier name was Narendra) went to Ramakrishna, who was the leading saint in his day. Narendra's heart was so hard that he did not even pay his respects to the saint, and very arrogantly put to Ramakrishna the question: "Have you seen God?" to which Ramakrishna replied, "Yes, I have seen him." Narendra then asked, "How did you see him?" He replied,

"As I see you." Narendra said, "Can you show me God?"
Ramakrishna said, "Yes, I will show him to you in due course."

After that Narendra stayed with Ramakrishna. One day they
went to bathe in the river. The saint asked Narendra to come
close to him and told him to dive under the water. The moment
he dived Ramakrishna pounced on him and forcibly held
Narendra under the water. Now this lean and thin boy, as he was
in those days, struggled hard to get out of the water to save his
breath and his life. The more he struggled, the more the saint
forcibly kept him under water, until with all his might he threw
his master off his shoulders and came out of the water. When, in
a very angry mood, he accused Ramakrishna of trying to drown
him, the saint smiled and replied, "Well, Narendra, if you could
develop the same strength of desire to see God as you had to
come out of the water, you would certainly be able to see God!"

Thus, all his master's mercy, care, and love melted the heart
of the young rebel. Later on he became one of the greatest ex-
ponents of the Vedanta philosophy in India and in the West.

So it is quite possible to melt the hearts of all those people
who, because of circumstances, have hearts which have become
hard. They simply need love and care, and reasonable discourse
which will help to melt their hearts.

THE BLIND PEOPLE AND THE ELEPHANT

In India the Vedas are supposed to be the most authoritative
collection of the scriptures. Everything has to be referred to the
Vedas. Only if it is supported by the Vedas can a system be
honoured in India. So everybody tries to look to the Vedas for

support. In the Vedas, and particularly the Upanishads, it says in one place that without knowledge it is not possible to attain liberation. All those people who are inclined to the intellectual way have always quoted this part of the Vedic text to show that nobody, whoever he may be, who has not learnt about the Absolute and mastered the knowledge thoroughly, can liberate his soul from the duality of birth and death.

Similarly, there are quotations given by devotional people, also taken from the Vedas, to show that without devotion no liberation is possible, and they say, "After all, knowledge is only a dry thing so what use is knowledge to anyone! It is only through devotion one can approach the Absolute—forget all knowledge and forget all activity!"

But the adherents of activity can also quote certain passages from the Vedas to show that unless you put the teaching into practice by performing right actions nothing will happen; for Self-realization arduous physical disciplines are required, so all your knowledge and devotion are of no use unless you express them in performing your day-to-day obligations.

Ordinary man hearing quotations from all these three sources usually gets perplexed, for he is neither fully capable of all activity, nor of all knowledge, nor can he fully devote himself to the Absolute because he has to live his householder's life. So it is necessary for anyone who has heard different views and become perplexed to enquire and get everything clear for his own sake. Here is an example:

Once an elephant appeared in a village; the news went around and everyone wanted to experience the elephant. Unfortunately most of the inhabitants were blind but still wanted to experience the elephant, so they were led to it. The mahout let them touch the elephant, and of course they each touched a different part. They then met to verify that they had experienced the real thing. The one who felt the foot said an elephant was a pillar, the one who had felt the tail said it was like a stick, and so it went on with the ears, trunk, tusks, belly, etc. Each person described it according to the type of previous experience to which he could relate it. Then they started arguing with each other: "Yours was not the proper elephant, yours was illusion, mine is the only real one, etc." Later on the mahout told them, "You cannot have a complete picture of the elephant. All you can do is put together all your different experiences of 'elephant,' and out of these experiences imagine a novel creature which is known as elephant, but it is the sum of all these parts and something more which represents the wholeness of the creature known as elephant."

In the same way, because of the different quotations from the scriptures, it is possible for some sort of conflict or doubt to arise in the minds of people. They must make an effort to find the truth, because there are people like this mahout, in our spiritual life, who are available to dispel doubts.

THE MAN WHO WANTED TO GO TO HIS FATHER-IN-LAW'S

Love is the motive force behind all the processes at work in the world to sustain it. The world could never be sustained without love. In the case of human life, examples are the love of parents, the love of brothers, the love of friends and colleagues, etc. Even the behaviour of insects and moths seems to be based on some form of love, so much so that the ultimate cause of hostility is also love, because hostility springs up when love is hindered. Thus a duality of love and hostility prevails everywhere. We want the thing that we love; if we do not get it, we turn hostile.

A love free from this duality is true love. The whole drama enacted by God depicts this one thing only. But there is no one to understand it.

A perennial game of hide-and-seek seems to be going on. We are all seeking something. Some seek it in annihilation, some in creation, some in light, some in darkness, some in intellect, etc. Actually it is God that all are seeking and God is hidden in all these and in everything else. But, while seeking, people have forgotten what they are actually seeking.

A man wanted to go to his father-in-law's place to meet his wife. He went to the railway station where the train was standing at the platform, and shouted at the booking clerk, "A ticket to my father-in-law's place, please!"

"Name of place, please!" insisted the booking clerk.

"Oh, my father-in-law's place! Please! Please! Quick!"

"Just tell me the name at once."

"I am telling you, my father-in-law's place. For God's sake, quick! the train is about to start!"

And the train started, leaving the man behind. Something like that is happening to all of us.

Ramana Maharshi meditated for fourteen years over the question: "Who am I?" As soon as he was on the right path, it took him only a minute to realize that he was everything.

When Rama was searching for Sita in the forest, he was so lost in his thoughts that he forgot everything about himself. He asked such questions of Lakshman: "Who am I? What is this? What is that? Where am I? How did I get here?"

When Lakshman reminded him, he collected his senses but soon lapsed into senselessness again. Over and over these questions were asked and answered, but forgotten again and again.

This is what is happening with all of us. In a state of perpetual forgetfulness, we are searching for something without finding it. We want to know what we are. We want to be happy, that is, we are seeking God. But God is in everything, though there is a curtain of ignorance between Him and us.

We should see God in everything. If we do that, we receive special favours from Him. Then this curtain of ignorance lifts, and illusion, which has been cheating us all the time—no longer does so and begins to help us instead.

When we have a sense of direction the work doesn't appear arduous. When we have lost this direction, when we do not know the way, then comes trouble. When we know the place we wish to go to and the route to it, then our journey becomes easy. If we do not know this then we experience a lot of difficulty.

RAMA—THE IDEAL MAN

The vernacular *Ramayana* was written by the great Hindi poet Tulasidas. The name of this is *Rama Charita Manasa*, which means that it describes the exploits of Rama, or the character of an ideal man, symbolised by Rama. This ideal man is not necessarily the story of a physical man, but in this story the physical man is entwined with the psychological and the divine man as well, and all the three aspects of our being—the physical, the subtle, and the spiritual are given in this book, and Rama stands as the symbol of the ideal man.

The story tells that when Rama was born at Ayodhya there were many other young boys born at the same time, and they all lived together. They had all joined in the wedding procession of the bridegroom with his parents, relatives and friends, and all the ministers. These young friends of Rama's complained to him saying that Rama was getting married without caring about them. He then promised that he would not get married unless all of them were married, so the young girls of Janak-Puri were prepared to marry all these young men from Ayodhya.

The significance of this marriage, which is the physical marriage, is also related to the spiritual realm. Rama here symbolises the Absolute and Sita (his bride-to-be) symbolises the fundamental nature; the marriage simply means the union, the coming together. This fundamental nature is also said to be the obedient wife of the Lord of Creation. The young men of Ayodhya represent the individual beings of this universe. The young girls of Janak-Puri are taken as the true knowledge or scriptures and these have to come together. Each individual has to acquire this purified knowledge, and bring himself and his wife to a state where the union of the Lord of Creation and nature takes place.

It also describes how the *sannyasins*, the holy men, came to take part in the procession. It is somewhat unusual for *sannyasins* to follow a marriage procession, so this calls for an explanation.

The reason given is that the king of Janak-Puri, the Janak, is also known as *videha*, a man who does not consider the physical world of much importance, a man who, though dwelling in his body, is not attached to it since he lives in the spirit.

Janaka is a state, a country, where with the prevalence of knowledge, the physical body does not have much importance, and this is possible only because true knowledge is being discussed there and practised in everyday life. So the holy men went there to experience this, how one could live in the body, inhabit the body, and yet not be bound by the body.

Although the story is being told of the physical realm, it also has the divine or spiritual behind it. In India it has been the tradition that, although the stories do talk of physical man and woman, they are all constructed in such a way that they tell the real story of the spirit and the Gods as well.

How the Original Shankaracharya Taught with the Help of Giri

According to human nature there are three types of people: the people who want to go on the way of action, those who prefer the way of knowledge, and those on the way of devotion. All of them have to perform certain activities. The man of action, if he has not prepared himself with knowledge and devotion, is very much like an animal. But the other two, the one who goes on the way of wisdom or knowledge, and the one on the way of devotion, prove that there are these two predominant ways everywhere, even in India. There are two camps, and they believe that the realization of the Self is possible by either way, and go accordingly; both of them are right to a certain extent.

It can be said with confidence that if one took up a mantra suitable for the achievement which one desired, and practised the mantra for the regulated time in the proper way, then one would achieve what one wanted to achieve, and one would be able to do whatever is enshrined in that mantra.

A man who wants to go on the way of knowledge can also acquire knowledge and become proficient. Such men are like land registrars who have all the maps and plans of the district and village farms, but cannot grow anything. Their papers are in no way productive.

Those on the devotional way have full faith and achieve realization by practice and experience, and may not need any knowledge, but if they have to explain the way to others they may not be able to do so, and vice versa—the man of knowledge only may not show anything in practice. However erudite a man may be, he may be able to explain everything in the minutest detail, but he will never be at all effective in moving the hearts of people. His heart is empty. There are available a number of experts who know all the scriptures and they can certainly speak much better than a monk or a saint can, but if you look deep into their life, it is almost empty of any spiritual quality.

But there are other examples where all these forces are brought together, just as in the life of the original Shankaracharya. He had the action, he had the wisdom and he had the devotion. Everything in full measure was seen to be active in the body of the first Shankaracharya.

The original Shankaracharya used to lead his disciples in Jyotir Math, and instruct them, and help their devotional practice as well. There was one of his disciples, called Giri, who was not at all concerned with the knowledge aspect but he was the greatest devotee of the Shankaracharya.

In the mornings the Shankaracharya used to conduct recitation and explanation of the scriptures, and all his disciples used to assemble for this purpose. One day Giri was very late and the other disciples became annoyed that there should be such a long delay in starting, just waiting for this stupid man who never bothered himself about knowledge. One of the disciples, Padma Pada, got annoyed, and said, "My lord, this man never bothers to understand or learn anything; he is very much like a beast who cares nothing about knowledge. Why should we waste our time in waiting for him to arrive?"

Then the Shankaracharya knew that this man, although erudite and fully informed, would denounce the way of devotion, so he wanted to teach him a lesson for all time.

When the ignorant disciple Giri was about to reach the hall, the Shankaracharya emanated his forces into him, and Giri started reciting one of the devotional writings which are credited to Trota Kachanya. When Giri came in reciting all these verses, everybody was astonished and enquired, "How can a man as stupid as Giri compose and recite such verses? Not only recite, but compose and recite original verses!"

Then the Shankaracharya explained that it is possible for the devotional man to inherit all knowledge, but such cases are very exceptional. It is very exceptional that everything is made available by one way only. The usual need is for unity between devotion and knowledge; both these have to work together and only then is something worthwhile possible; particularly for this age, devotion alone is not going to achieve much. Devotion and knowledge are equally needed, so that one can be effective.

THE TWO ARTISTS

When the Shankaracharya speaks of offering one's actions, everything one has, to God, does this apply to both intellectual and devotional types of people or is it particular to one?

Surrender is necessary for all three types (men predominantly of action, knowledge, or devotion), because unless you surrender, you will not find light shed even for an intellectual understanding of things. Surrender is necessary for devotion and faith, of course.

Here is a story which will clarify the difference between the intellectual and devotional paths:

Two artists visiting a particular state went to the king and said, "We are artists and would like to display our art; the beauty of our art is that both of us will depict the same thing." The king said, "That is not very difficult, you will copy each other!" So they said, "Give us just one room, but partition it in the middle; one man will work in his part of the room, and the other man will work in the other part, and ultimately you will find that both of us will produce the same." The king was intrigued and arranged it.

A room was allotted and partitioned down the centre. One half was given to one artist, the other half to the other. After cleaning the wall the first artist started to sketch a very beautiful figure on it. The other man just cleaned the wall—to do this he rubbed and rubbed and rubbed, polishing it so much that it started to reflect whatever was in front of it. Then the partition was removed, the light was put on, and it was seen that the sketch made by one was reflected perfectly on the wall of the other! The same thing could be seen.

Now, the one who sketched was a devotee and the one who polished was an intellectual. In other words, the intellectual reflects the ultimate, while the devotee creates the ultimate.

If one could take the analogy further, can devotion be seen as the love of what is being sketched?

Yes, love plays a part there. An intellectual considers that there is nothing except God. The approach of devotion is that everything is God.

Even a man who takes to the way of knowledge has some initial devotion as well, to give him the momentum to go deeper into the enquiry. Although he may not realize he has some devotion in him, yet it is a spark of devotion which sets him on the way. He wants to understand an aspect of God so that he can see the transcendent reality in the form of knowledge.

If you take the other way, the way of devotion, even there the devotee must have some knowledge of what he wants to unite with; it may not be full knowledge, but he must have some knowledge of God in order to go deeper or further on the way of devotion. The closer he comes to God, the beloved, the more he exhibits everything that his beloved has.

It is the play of the drama which God has created which is being manifested.

The way of devotion is the manifestation, or the illustration in action, by the devotee of whatever glory of God he has, and the act of knowledge is to perceive by analysis whatever is within that illustration. In fact they both go towards the same point from two different directions. Having reached the destination it happens naturally that the devotee, having fully realized the union, wants to see all aspects of God, so he turns to knowledge. The one who has gone through knowledge wants to experience all the aspects of God, so he turns to devotion. In both cases the end will be exactly the same.

To achieve any permanent result you need a system of philosophy, such as Advaita, and one must follow each step to achieve the required result.

In the yoga system of Patanjali the body and intellect are progressively trained for control over the senses and the moving mind. Thus one has to learn to regulate one's activities and obey certain rules of conduct: to sit quietly and properly without making much movement, and regulate the breathing; to relinquish all worldly thoughts and hold one idea in the mind; only then is one allowed to meditate. The yoga system of Patanjali, with its eight steps, is a hard system and only the brave can follow it even with a good guide.

The meditation is a simpler way of covering the same steps which still have to be accomplished.

It is not the system which bothers people, but the lack of it. They wish to be free, and yet want results. How can they get anything without working for it? They must learn control. Nature is refined and beautified only by control and systematic practice, not by doing whatever you feel like.

The yoga system is like the painting in the story of the two artists, while our meditation is like the polishing. The result is the same, but both have a system of their own. Both produce the result, and both need work and attention. If meditation is done properly, all the activities of that individual will be automatically controlled and balanced. If they are not controlled and balanced he is not meditating properly.

I am very interested in visualisation—it plays a big part in my job as a designer. It appears to me to consist of seeing into the future, or bringing the future into the present. I don't believe this faculty is in any way restricted to creative activities, but also plays a big part in everyone's ordinary life. Is it possible to perform an intentional act without first visualising it? Is this a form of memory?

There are two aspects of the creative activity of the Absolute, one which manifests itself and the other which withdraws itself. The creative act of manifestation is what you are talking about. This act is rightly performed only if the artist is healthy, in the sense that he is empty, he is not attached, and everything about him is pure. Then he looks at, and into, this wonderful creation, elicits all the information he needs and puts everything together in such a way that it makes a good piece of art.

Reverse this creative process and you have meditation; in meditation everything we have collected is gradually eliminated and we go deeper and deeper to where there is nothing except the creative force, the Self. One is the art of manifestation, artistic work, and the other is the art of going deep into the Self, which is meditation. These are the two aspects of the creativity of the Absolute.

The two aspects of the creative act are shown in the story of the two artists. One is the meditation, which is polishing, bringing in the brilliance of the Absolute by elimination, so it can reflect everything purely and accurately without distortion. The other is the art which we have to learn in the physical world. When you visualise you take in the qualities of the Absolute; if you are empty, not possessed by anything, then you will embark on the creative act with the proper attitude.

12

Meditation, Prayer, and Stillness

NO AUDIENCE TODAY

How can one get rid of ego in one's feeling when one knows one is approaching the centre? One bounces off the place of transcendence when one knows one is getting near it.

One should look forward to unity with faith, enthusiasm, and love. With patience and determination your real Self will take you into the centre and let your ego drop away.

There was a realized man who had plenty of disciples of all types; they used to flock round him every day to see him and get his blessing. He used to test his disciples in rather a peculiar way. He would close the doors one day and the attendant would tell all the disciples, "No audience today."

Most of them would go away, but a few would stay on and sit there, and after a long time he would have the doors opened and ask how many there were. Even if only a few were there he would ask them to come in and would hold his audience.

THE MAN WHO WANTED A BLACK HORSE

The law of three prevails at every stage and is involved in every event of life. There isn't anything which escapes the law of three. The same law of three is described as physical, subtle, and causal. It applies to three types of rest, and also to three *gunas* (qualities or energies) which are *sattva* (purity or light), *rajas* (agitation, excitement), and *tamas* (inertia or darkness). Whatever event you choose and visualise or analyse you will find the law of three governs it. In relation to the ego, each individual who has a unified concept of himself and a picture evolving out of this unified concept of the world as he sees it, and the way he behaves, is governed by this law of three. If the person is lethargic, then everything appears to be composed of negative elements and he sees the world in a negative way. Similarly with an excitable or peaceful person.

The same can be seen in worship. If the worship is *tamasic* people practise peculiar disciplines to control evil forces, ghosts, etc.; they perform certain rituals and keep on doing this for a long time so that they can acquire the power to dictate their desires to these evil forces and make sure they are fulfilled.

The *rajasic* type of worship is mostly related to different gods. There are a variety of gods in a hierarchy under the Absolute, and some people try to please these gods by devotional acts and rituals, and thus gain their favour so that their desires may be fulfilled.

However, the man who worships with *sattva* attends only to the Absolute. Accordingly he will acquire great powers. He does not look at the result, and he does not have any particular desires. These are the three ways showing the law of three working through worship or devotion.

We can see the same thing in relation to thought, action, and sleep. A really healthy man needs only a few hours' sleep, and after that he should be happy enough to perform all sorts of vigorous physical or intellectual work. But there are people who keep on sleeping for hour after hour—over eight or ten hours—and even after that they are not very ready to get out of bed! They keep on desiring more sleep; it never gives them any more rest and never gives them any more power, but this is the way they waste their lives in sloth.

Restless, or *rajasic*, sleep is when you keep on having all sorts of worries in your mind and keep on dreaming, or creating dreams and weaving desires and plans for achievements so that you waste the whole time that you intend to sleep and you never get any rest and keep engaging in further activity.

Peaceful, or *sattvic*, sleep is when you go to sleep at once, the moment you are in bed, and after a few hours you are fully fresh and awake so that you can attend to everything that is necessary. There we have the law of three related to the being or attitude of the individual through which he activates himself in relation to the world.

Again, in relation to *samadhi* the law of three prevails.

There was a particular man who had trained himself in physical *samadhi*. He went to the king and said he wanted a black horse. He said to the king that he would demonstrate his *samadhi*, lasting twelve years, and as a reward for this exemplary *samadhi* he would like to have the black horse from the king's stables. The king agreed and all the necessary arrangements for his *samadhi* were made. A trench was dug and he was placed in it. It was covered with planks and soil. Then everybody forgot about him.

Some time during these twelve years the king died and so did the horse. But the desire of the man in *samadhi* remained alive, because he was neither asleep nor dead, he was in *samadhi*. The whole situation in the kingdom changed after twelve years. Some people in the kingdom were building a new palace at the *samadhi* site. When they came across the man in *samadhi* they dug him out. When he regained consciousness he asked for his black horse. "What black horse?" they asked. He asked for the king and asked them to call him. They told him the king was dead. Then he explained that the old king had agreed to give him his black horse after twelve years of *samadhi* which he had now completed. Could he please now have that black horse? He was then told that the horse was also dead so he could now have nothing.

This was an example of *tamasic samadhi* as there was something which the man wanted to acquire after twelve years of non-activity or non-productive *samadhi*.

There is *rajasic samadhi* when you get peace after doing some activity. After a little peace you once again hurry into activity and keep on with this cycle of activity and peace. It keeps you going but it does not improve the situation, though of course there may not be any loss either.

As an example of *sattvic samadhi* there is the *Rasleela* (divine play). The Lord Krishna as a youth used to dance with the shepherdesses in the jungles of Mathura, and one of the pictures that we have been given is that of the dance coming to the end; at the final stage all the shepherdesses stand in a circle and between every two shepherdesses there is one Krishna. This picturesque view of the *Rasleela* shows that between two activities, the shepherdesses, is the restful Krishna, the Absolute, and this is the symbol which has been adopted to form this *Rasleela*.

This represents the rest that we ought to have after each activity so that we can initiate the next activity with a better understanding and with our inner forces more readily available.

As far as the thought process is concerned, the peaceful person just listens and understands the content and form of what is said. The active person listens sometimes and gets some partial view, and the lethargic person either falls asleep or into a trance and misses everything or immediately forgets whatever he has heard. He retains nothing or misunderstands it.

Akbar and the Jackals

All living beings seem to be crying out for something or other. Among mankind some pray for wealth, some for health, some for property, some for fame, some for power, some for freedom from troubles, some for food and the basic necessities of life. Moreover, all want what they ask for to be given on a permanent basis; nobody wants merely a temporary cure or temporary riches. Also we want these things in full measure, and nothing less is good enough, our object being to make and keep ourselves fulfilled in all respects.

The scriptures belonging to every religion devote thought to the question of what among all these things is really worth praying for. If we study those scriptures accessible to us, it would seem as if all of them want God because it is only He who is complete in all respects and His fullness can never decrease.

All the rest are neither complete nor permanent. Thus, people really seem to be wanting God though they do not realize this.

When one is a child, one wants toys; when one is a boy, one wants education; when one's education is over, one wants employment; when one gets employment, one wants promotion. Thus, from the beginning to the end, one is never content.

Once, the great Moghul emperor Akbar had to spend the night in the jungle while out hunting. Unable to sleep owing to the noise made by jackals, he asked why they were crying. Someone said it was on account of the cold. Akbar ordered blankets to be distributed to the jackals, but still they went on crying. When Akbar again asked the reason, he was told that it was on account of their joy at getting the blankets!

In this way satisfaction in stillness and peace never comes to us, and we continue to cry!

The remedy is devoting yourself to God. With this all the unnecessary thinking of worldly needs comes to an end and this is succeeded by realization of the Universal Self. Only then is there complete satisfaction; wanting nothing, we feel fulfilled. A union takes place between the complete Self and the Universal Self. These two aspects mingle inseparably, and are never again divided.

Though God manifests Himself in everything, everything suffers some kind of distortion, yet God Himself cannot be distorted, just as gold remains gold even after being shaped and reshaped a thousand times into various ornaments. As long as we do not know God, our belief in Him remains half-hearted; only when we know Him does our belief become firm and unshakeable.

STHITAPRAJNA AND STILLNESS

The time spent during meditation is in preparation to lead one to the state of stillness. There may be meditators who sit for hours and hours but to no avail, because they keep on churning their mechanical thoughts in habitual rotation. They end up tired, both physically and mentally. Those who manage to dive deep come out with potentiality emanating from the will of the Absolute.

In the *Mahabharata*, Arjuna asked Shri Krishna about the man with such stillness. In the *Bhagavad-Gita*, such a man is called Sthitaprajna, 'one who is steady and still in his knowledge and being.' Krishna says that such a man is not agitated though in discomfort, pain, or misery. He does not rise in revolt against such misfortune. Even if a calamity befalls him, he neither gives up nor feels sorry; he attends only to overcoming its effects with a smile. When honoured with success, pleasure, or comfort he never expresses jubilation; he simply accepts them with gratitude, and then forgets them. In short, one could say that a man with this profound stillness always remains the same and expresses efficiency, wisdom, love, and mercy.

That proves that this immobility or stillness must be ever present; therefore, in truth, it would seem that meditation starts there?

It is rather that this stillness is itself the real experience of meditation. Since there is no movement, one cannot call it a starting point, for nothing is starting. When one comes out of such a state, then one comes out with the treasure, and this treasure is without end. In ordinary rest and stillness, one regains only some of one's lost energy, but, having reached this stillness, one is never without energy and love. Such a man always does everything as if fresh, new and for the first time. This is because his body, mind, intelligence, feelings, and emotions come together in unity to face any situation. Whenever he tackles a problem, all his forces work through this one-pointed attention.

THE MAHATMA AND THE TAMARIND TREE

The process of giving importance to, say, the meditation and also to the idea of the goodness of the Absolute seems to give more power to work wonders. The same idea is at the beginning of the Lord's Prayer of the Christians: "Our Father in heaven, we pray that Thy Name be made holy." Through the Shankaracharya both the Absolute and the meditation have become 'holy' for many people and then they work wonders. How can we enter more fully into this enjoyable task?

Whenever someone completely or partially experiences unity the usual wish is to share it with others and the same feeling is shown by this question. This is a natural process. There are difficulties, not for the man who wants to share, but for those who could share in what he has to offer because they have certain barriers. These barriers have to be broken and for that there are ways prescribed.

Good company is one of the ways. It is good to bring people together and then in front of them describe all the beautiful things, the glorious aspects of the Absolute, in such a way that all the barriers in those people are broken down gradually so that they can respond much more fully. This is the best way to carry out this work. Unless people understand that there is something better they will not move in that direction, so this imparting of the knowledge of the glory of the Absolute is essential and people should be brought together where such discussions are possible.

As for prayer, there are two types. One describes the glorious aspects of the Absolute, and the poet does it in a beautiful form, speaking of everything which the Absolute has manifested in different ways in this world. The other way is to remove the power of the ego, and in this sort of prayer one does not speak about the glory of God, but about one's own shortcomings, so one says that one is not capable of doing this, one has done this wrong and that wrong, and asks the Absolute to be merciful and to save one from all these vices.

Although there are these two ways, the better way is the first, where one speaks about the glory of the Absolute. Although by the other way the ego is reduced, nothing very positive is put in its place so, although this way is not inferior, the glory does not immediately descend on one.

By the first sort of prayer, one says that the Absolute, God, is all-knowing, all-pervading, has all the forces in the world, has created a beautiful world in all its forms, and because one is his son, one would also like to enjoy everything which he has created, and also partake in the creative act, just as a lion cub in the course of time acts like a fully grown lion. But by the other way one keeps on saying to the Absolute, as is said in one of the Sanskrit prayers: "I am a sinner, and I have been indulging myself in sinful activities, and I am very lowly; would you please be kind enough to deliver me from these things, will you please forgive me for being like that." Ultimately, you see that a prayer which goes towards the glory aspect is much more positive, much more rewarding.

There was a saint living in a secluded place under a tamarind tree. He performed his devotional act of meditation every day. There is a deity known as Narada who is supposed to be the messenger of the Absolute and keeps on descending to earth to gather information to keep the Absolute fully and well informed. He happened to be making his rounds when he came near this saint and engaged in conversation with him, wanting to know what he was doing.

The saint said, "Well, this is all a drama and at the moment I am engaged in the drama of meditation, and who are you?" Narada replied that he was the messenger of the Absolute and was collecting information about all the devotees of God so that he could inform Him about their well-being. The saint said this was excellent, as he could take a message and Narada said, "Yes, why not?" The saint said, "Ask Him when I will meet Him."

Narada went away, and after some time returned and the saint asked him if there was any reply. Narada said that there was a reply, but it was rather a bitter one and he would rather not give it as the saint's heart would sink. The saint said, "But if there is any reply from the Absolute, my heart would never sink, so don't worry about it, just let me know the answer."

Narada said, "Look at this tree, the tamarind tree. It has very small leaves, and millions of them. As many leaves as there are on this tree you will have to wait the same number of years, after which God will come to meet you; this is the message."

At this the saint became ecstatic and started dancing with bliss, completely forgetting himself. Narada was quite baffled by this man, who when told he had to wait millions of years before the union could take place, yet was dancing with joy. He said, "Wait—did you really understand what I said? What does my answer imply to you?" The saint said, "Yes, I heard," and Narada said, "What did you hear?" and the saint said, "As many leaves as there are on the tamarind tree, that many years will I have to wait and then He will come." Narada said, "Well, why are you dancing?" The saint said, "I am not going to count the number of years and the leaves; all that matters is that I have had a message from the Absolute, and He is going to meet me; He will never let me down, that is what really matters," and once again he started dancing.

Narada wondered what was happening, and at that moment the Absolute Himself descended and embraced the saint and appeared before him. Narada was very disturbed. He said, "My Lord, I am Your messenger, but don't let me be proved a liar because You said it would be so many years, and that is what I told the saint, and You have broken Your word and descended immediately! You didn't even wait an hour and You've fulfilled the promise which was supposed to wait for years."

Then the Absolute said, "These things are for ordinary men; if there is somebody special, then the question of time and space has to be satisfied and the meeting must be instantaneous."

The same applies to all these details about people of devotion or people of knowledge. If there is a rare case where there is nothing else—only devotion, or where there is nothing but a longing for truth—then the union can take place without any delay.

TULASIDAS AND THE BOY TRYING TO CROSS THE RIVER

Is it the mantra that purifies the causal level or soul and how does the mantra receive this power? Is it the sound of the mantra, or the fact that it has been given from a tradition, or is it the purity of heart of the meditator?

The sound of the mantra has been given to us through the Vedic tradition, and its roots are in Brahman, the Absolute, itself. All these pure sounds which are incorporated in the mantra are full of qualities and each sound has a particular element or meaning, which combine to create a particular type of effect when the mantra is being repeated by the individual. Thus the meaning of the mantra and its proper pronunciation by the meditator internally will have the proper effect which is embodied in the sound of the mantra itself.

It does three types of work. First of all it eliminates all the impure, unnecessary, and harmful traits in the individual, or in his soul or causal level, and secondly it increases and develops whatever good he holds within himself. There is also a process of expansion which takes place on the causal level so that he becomes much more universal, appreciates the universe more, and becomes more united and in tune with it. These are the three factors which crystallise through the mantra.

As far as the individual is concerned, certainly purity of heart is a good precondition for the mantra to work much better than it would with an impure heart. So although the mantra is the same, when given to different types of people it produces an effect according to their capacity, based on the purity of heart of the individual. Some people get the result much more quickly, while others get it later and there may be cases where no result is seen and perhaps in frustration they may give up the meditation and the mantra. The third factor concerns the tradition. The tradition makes a mantra much more potent because it has been evolved through the centuries and millennia and been practised by great saints, and the forces of these saints have been passed from one to another, from teacher to disciple. So there is this third type of force which comes through the tradition.

The saint Tulasidas who wrote the vernacular *Ramayana* used to live in Benares and while he was sitting on the banks of the Ganges a small boy came crying to the river bank one evening. He had come to the city to get medicine for his sick mother who was in the town across the river. At that time there were no boats available as all the boatmen had gone home. The boy was crying because he was unable to cross to the other bank and didn't know what to do about his ailing mother and her medicine. The saint heard the boy crying and came down to ask what troubled him. The boy told his story. The saint then gave the little boy a leaf, on which was written a mantra, and he told him to hold it in his palm and swim across the river. He would then have no difficulty in getting across. The boy was very curious and thought he would like to see what had been given to him. He opened the leaf and saw the word written on it. He thought, well, I know this word myself and there is no difference between this word I have been given and my own, so I can cross myself. When he tried to swim he found himself swept away by the force of the water. When the saint saw what was happening he said, "But my dear boy, your word is not going to help you. You ask for help from my mantra. So take the leaf and hold on to it." The boy took his advice and crossed the river.

Although things may seem to be the same, when a mantra comes from a tradition it has certain potent forces.

HOW VALMIKI BECAME ENLIGHTENED

In meditation once the body becomes very still, this seems to make every-thing so much easier. This very still state of the body seems to be a big key in meditation.

The *Bhagavad-Gita*, which consists of the words of Lord Krishna, says one has to be still and comfortable, in a relaxed position.

Brahma is one of our Lords, Brahma, Vishnu, and Shiva. Brahma is the Creator. His son was Prajekitas, whose son was Valmiki. Valmiki was the first poet in Sanskrit. But before he became a poet, he got into bad company. He was a householder with children who met his own needs and those of his family by stealing things and by killing people and looting.

Once he stopped some holy men to rob them. The leader of the holy men said to Valmiki, "Although we have very little to give, we will give you everything if you answer one question. You kill and rob people to support your dependents. They share your loot, but are you sure they are prepared to share the consequences of your sins as well?" Valmiki went home and asked them. His family replied, "We are your responsibility and depend upon you for our food and life, but we don't want you to kill and rob others for us. You could work to support us. Why do you do wrong things to feed us? Do only good things. You love to sin so that is your business and we are not going to share in the result of your bad deeds!"

That opened his eyes, and he came back to the holy men and said, "Tell me something by which I can be free of my sins and improve my future." These holy men then told him to sit down and gave him a mantra. Although he did not find it easy to repeat the mantra, he got so absorbed in it that he sat still and this stillness became meditation. He became so engrossed in it that in about a year his entire body was covered in clay. Ants made their home in the clay. He didn't feel them because he was engrossed in something else. He was so still that he didn't mind what had happened to his body. After a year, the holy men came again and removed the clay and they found that he was fully enlightened.

They said, "Now you have become perfect." After that he developed the power of seeing into the future, and he wrote the *Ramayana* even before Rama was born.

From this one can conclude that it is the sitting still which is the key.

THE THREE LEAPS OF THE FROG

When we meditate together there is a general feeling of greater physical stillness but individuals say that although they get this physical stillness more quickly now, they still find much movement in their minds, and they ask how to reach the deep peace more quickly, and stay there longer?

The achievement of physical stillness is not an ordinary thing in itself; it is a very important achievement. There are three factors which come together as far as the meditation is concerned—the body, the eyes, and the mind. When the body is totally still, the next movement is found in the eyes which will keep on flickering, however slightly. When the eyes are still, it is most probable that the mind will follow suit. Mind moves according to the movement of the body, and there are other factors, but body first, eyes next, will be followed peacefully by the mind.

Meditation, as it has been given to you, starts with the body, and the training of the body to become still is the first stage of entry into the spiritual world. There should not be much difficulty in achieving the stillness of the mind in due course.

There is a sage who wrote the *Mandukya Upanishad. Mandukya* is a word which really means 'frog' and this sage, who had evolved a system, said that with three leaps one could reach the deepest level of the Self. A frog who happens to be on dry land and is getting burned by the sun, and wants to be cool and peaceful, can jump into the water with three leaps where he can enjoy the cool and peace of the deepest water. Similarly, these are the three leaps we need, and with these three leaps it should be possible to establish the stillness of the mind.

THE TORTOISE AND THE HARE

Why is it that immediately one congratulates oneself one falls flat on one's face?

The satisfaction acquired by extra effort usually creates a sense of achievement; having achieved something, it is possible that you feel you can rest on your laurels for a while. It is said, "Rest prunes progress," and the fall is very near! Here is an illustration:

There is a children's story that a tortoise and a hare set out to win a race. The hare ran very fast and quickly covered a great distance. Looking back he couldn't see the tortoise anywhere. Thinking that the tortoise would take a long time to get as far as that, the hare sat down to rest. He slept so soundly that the tortoise managed to reach the destination before the hare woke up. The tortoise, who does the two half-hours meditation conscientiously, will get there in the end, whereas the hare may not!

13

Laws

THE MAN DRIVING THE FOUR-HORSE CARRIAGE

*Does your teaching agree that the modern world is governed by the law of
chance or accident?*

The scientific world, or the modern world of today, sees a
law of chance or accident everywhere and believes that the
world is usually governed by it. In fact, there is nothing like a
law of chance. It is the ignorant who cannot see the law, and take
it as chance. People who have wisdom and experience know the
law, and know how and when this law is going to affect them.

During the time of the British Raj, there was a law under
which only certain high officials of the government or kings and
nawabs of a certain rank with permits were allowed to drive on
the high road in a carriage drawn by four horses. There was a
man who built carriages and dealt in horses. One day he drove
a carriage which he had just built, with four horses, without
knowing about the law. He was stopped by the police and asked
whether he had a permit, but he said he was just trying out the

carriage. He was issued with a summons and he became frightened and worried about the punishment. He consulted lawyers but they said he had certainly infringed the law and would be punished and so they would not take on his case.

However, there was an old and experienced lawyer who listened to his story and then asked to see the carriage and horses. He inspected these very carefully and then said that he would take on the case. The man would have to pay one thousand rupees, but the lawyer would get him acquitted. He told the man to come to court in the same carriage and driven by exactly the same four horses as he had used when he was summonsed. The man was very frightened at repeating the offence but the lawyer said he would take full responsibility.

When the prosecution had presented the case, the defending lawyer asked the judge to inspect the carriage himself and also the four horses. When the inspection was over, the lawyer pointed out that the law said the carriage must not be driven by four horses, but in fact there were three mares and only one horse, therefore his client had not broken the law and there was no case to answer. The law said nothing about mares! The man was set free but the law was later changed to cover both mares and horses!

To the ignorant the law appears to be chance, but to a man of knowledge it is not chance but law, the same law of cause and effect which works throughout creation. It is only for the ignorant that the law appears to be concealed, but in reality consciousness prevails through the law which may be subtle or coarse. The man who lives in the coarse world cannot see the law which originates in the subtle world and so calls it the law of chance.

*What I mean by the law governing numbers is a very precise mathematic-
al law according to which, if you have, say, a million ants collected at
random in a heap, a certain number would like only sugar, and an equal
number would like only salt, but in between these extremes the vast major-
ity of average ants might like one or the other or both from time to time.
The law is exact, but chance is said to determine what will happen to any
individual ant.*

To look for the law of chance or the law of large numbers
is to look away from consciousness. There are those in the world
who have less consciousness, just as one can see in the whole
hierarchy of beings in the universe that men have more consciousness than animals, animals more than plants and minerals which have very little consciousness, but everywhere
consciousness prevails. In fact, everything is conscious; it is only
the law of consciousness which differs. Nothing moves without
consciousness and consciousness does not move by chance; it
moves by law—the law of cause and effect. If one adheres to
the law of chance one is depriving oneself of the law of consciousness.

You will remember the story of the two groups of ants which
eat salt and sugar and how the group who are trying the taste of
sugar had to go on till all the taste of salt had left them before
they could get the real full taste of the sugar. When they had
really tasted the sugar, they did not want salt any more.

On the human level, ignorant people who like living in
their ignorance do not want to appreciate consciousness. Because they cannot give up their old habit of always looking to
the physical world, it is very hard for them to appreciate that

even if the law is not obvious, there is a proper law working through everything. They simply have to rise to a better level and see the law for themselves through their own consciousness.

Are there any practices other than the meditation which would help our endeavours?

It is not necessary to have many practices, many ways of practice. For example: You pass a law degree and then you start practising. Now when you practise you gain experience. A person with one year's practice will have less experience than someone with fifteen years' practice. But you don't have to pass law finals again and again. You have passed them already and by your practising in the courts you get a certain experience.

Similarly in meditation, once you have learnt the theory and method of meditation you practise it. You don't have to go on practising something else as well. As it goes deeper and deeper, your experience will be increased. So you don't have to change practices or acquire new practices.

In the story of the carriage drawn by four horses the knowledge of law was the same for all the lawyers, but it was the older lawyer's power of observation which he had developed by virtue of his long practice that made the difference.

By continual practice, you will acquire that aptitude which will be helpful in getting what you want, not by changing the method of practice.

THE LAME MAN AND THE BLIND MAN

In New York people asked me why I had to go to India, so far away? I told them it was not geographical. I knew what I wanted, and if I could have found it nearer home it would have been more convenient. I went on to mention the Shankaracharya's example of the lame man and the blind man. Would the Shankaracharya have suggested something better?

According to Indian tradition this story is related to natural law and man-made law. Man-made law is not far-sighted. Natural law does not have the capacity to command because it simply moves naturally, whereas man-made law commands, demands, and makes people follow it. The relation between them is like that between husband and wife. If both agree there is peace, prosperity, and contentment. But if there is conflict between husband and wife there will never be much peace in the house, just eternal conflict.

The men who understand the natural laws and the men who administer the man-made laws are, respectively, like a lame man who can see but cannot move, and a blind man who is very active but cannot see in what direction he is going or what will be the consequences of his actions.

A way must be found for these two kinds of people to work together. The blind man should take the lame man on his shoulders. The lame man advises the blind man which way to walk, and the blind man can get around, but if there is conflict nothing can be done—the blind man will run the wrong way and the lame man can only talk.

This should be the relation of holy or spiritual leaders

to public men—men of business or government. If this relationship were established and maintained, the house of the nation would have peace. Otherwise the nation eventually disintegrates.

THE JUDGE WHO WAS INJURED IN A CAR ACCIDENT

The chief difficulty for many people is that they see all kinds of tragedies which they cannot understand and this drives many people away from God. What can one say to such people?

One has to understand two facets here, one is universal and the other is individual; the presiding deity of the universal is God himself and the person responsible for the individual is the individual himself. There are two sets of laws that apply to the government of these two levels. The laws which govern the individual are the outcome of the actions of that individual through the cycles of birth and death. The reward for the deeds which he has performed in his previous life will be presented to him in this life.

For instance, one might be going along the street and be involved in an accident and fall dead or be seriously injured. Obviously there is nothing to indicate the responsibility of the individual for being knocked down in the street. The only causal explanation that could be given for such accidents is that he might have done something in his previous life which is affecting him now.

There was a judge living in Benares. Being a well-read person and having been appointed a judge, he did not have much respect for the religious life, nor for God, and though living in Benares which is the main seat of Vishvanath, the Lord Shiva, he never believed in him so he never went to pay his respects to Shiva. But his mother was a very religious and pious soul; she always tried to impress on him that he should come with her once to the Vishvanath temple. But the judge always said he was a busy man with so many things to do, and these religious observances were for ignorant people, so that they could go and pray to Shiva, but he had nothing to do with him, and since he was busy he couldn't go.

One Sunday, his mother insisted that as it was Sunday he had no business to attend to, so he should come with her. She pressed him, and as an obedient son he followed his mother.

They were going towards the temple in their car, and just before they were to alight there was an accident in which the judge was hurt. He was not badly injured, but because of his injuries he became very agitated and blamed his mother for having involved him in this horrible accident because of her insistence that he accompany her. He called for a doctor and he was bandaged. During the night, he had a dream. In this dream the Lord Shiva appeared and told him, "You silly man, you were destined to have a bad accident, and some of your limbs would have been broken. A serious accident was to befall you because of the misdeeds of your previous life, but because your mother insisted on bringing you to my door, your sentence was reduced and you were given a small penalty. Had you not come here this Sunday, you would have been in hospital for months and months."

So when he got up next morning he went to his mother,

apologised, and put his head on her feet, and ever after he was a believer in the existence of God.

This set of laws is there to govern the individual and they will keep on operating; whatever happens is the reward for one's own deeds. One should understand these laws and then the misery following any seeming misfortune would be reduced.

Then there are the laws which govern large numbers within the universe. For instance, fifty people might be sitting in a boat and the boat might sink in the river, and one cannot say that all fifty deserve the same fate. There might be one who deserves it or none, but this is at the level of the universal where other forces are involved. Because of the activity on the universal level all these things happen: trains collide and hundreds of people die; a war comes and thousands of people die; at the frontier the forces from two different nations face each other and shoot and kill each other. This does not come about because of the deeds of the individual—although for everything that happens on either level, payment has to be made by individuals everywhere.

The presiding deity of the universal level is the Universal Self, but it responds with neither sorrow nor pleasure. So far as it is concerned it is only a play, a drama which is being enacted, and it is not involved in the justice of what is being performed, but it must act because the laws are there and its laws must be carried out. Since it comes back to the individual either on the individual level or on the universal level, the need for understanding is doubly necessary.

If one understands these two sets of laws, then one refrains from attaching oneself to whatever result occurs in life, either from oneself or as part of the universal laws of nature.

Just as in a drama, the individual actor, having performed

all the different actions, remains the same when off-stage, having no attachment of any sort, and does not react to the pleasures or misery of the drama on the stage. This is all one has to understand. If one understands these two sets of laws and detaches oneself from the resulting miseries and sorrows, then one can simply live according to the laws, both of which are regulated by the Absolute.

In the universe, there will never be a time when everything will go smoothly. In the nature of things there will always be some agitation and change, for the creation itself is the product of agitation or movement. There will be imbalance all the time. But for the individual there is a way of escape from this agitated state of the universe, and that is, as has been suggested to you all, in the meditation. Having gone deep into meditation you come to a state of equilibrium where the laws do not affect you—they do not touch you. That is the only moment of equilibrium available, apart from deep sleep, otherwise there will always be disturbances in the universe and we ought to learn to face them with detachment so that their effect in misery, ecstasy, or pleasure does not bind us.

14

Offering and Consistency

SERVE GOD WITH YOUR OWN ATTRIBUTES

There is something or other in all of us which is special or out-standing. For example, some are intelligent, some are not, some are strong and some are weak, some are learned and some are ignorant, some are rich and some are poor.

Each should try to please God, to serve God or worship God, as the case may be, with that attribute in which he chiefly excels. This is the path of least resistance. It is sure to work, as it has always done in the past.

Sudama was the poorest of the poor. He worshipped Krishna with rotten rice only, and that too was borrowed, because he was so poor. But this worship worked and Sudama got great wealth in return.

Little things can have great consequences. In fact, all great things begin from something little.

A tiny seed of the babul (a thorny tree in India) will produce a large thorny tree, and then this will produce innumerable others till the whole place becomes full of them and nobody can move through them without getting hurt.

Similarly, a small wrong action can cause much harm and a little good action just the opposite.

Kubja, a hump-backed woman who lived at the time of Krishna, worshipped Krishna by offering only very little sandalwood paste, but with total sincerity. All her troubles disappeared, and the hump also went. She became a beautiful woman. Her action was small, but her sincerity was great, therefore this miracle happened. Similarly, many stories in the scriptures illustrate the fact that even the lowest can reach the greatest heights.

The method is to do what each of you is meant for, and do it in a spirit of service to God. Let eating, drinking, sleeping, bathing, etc., all be dedicated to God. This is the correct worship and the correct devotion.

Shabari, an uneducated woman who lived at the time of the *Ramayana*, worshipped for a hundred years with full faith that the personification of God would visit her hut in the jungle one day, and this actually happened. Rama went to her hut during his exile. Though she was illiterate, her dedication was of a higher order than that even of mahatmas. Therefore Rama visited her hut and not theirs.

A strong and deep affection lives in our heart for our son or father or wife, yet we go about our normal business and do not recite their names all the time. This is exactly how we should keep God in our heart and go on doing our duty at the same time.

Do your normal duty in service to God and worship of God. You can reach God through it. But if you think that your own duties are no good and take up other people's duties because they appeal to you more, you can lose your way and ruin yourself. Thus, doing your own duty and dedicating it to God is the golden rule for peace and happiness.

RAMA AND SITA

The Shankaracharya spoke of consistency. Is it this that can provide the thread of memory through the day and keep a little light in the darkness?

There is a verse in one of the scriptures. The gist of it is that a good man who wants to go on the spiritual path says what he feels, and does what he says. That is, he speaks from pure feeling. When he has impure feelings, he tries not to speak or rush into action or express them. A bad man does the reverse: he feels one thing and says something else; he says something but does something else.

If one really did speak what one felt, and did exactly what one said, then this would build up the inner strength of the man and, because of this clarity and unity of his mind and sincerity of his heart, the way would be fairly clear for him.

There is an example from the life of Rama when he went to Janak-Puri. He was taking a stroll in the royal gardens and he happened to see Sita there. He had only Lakshman with him so he said to Lakshman, "Why is it that I had a glimpse of this girl in this garden? The tradition of our great family of Raghu is that no man of this family should ever have a glimpse of any woman unless he is destined to marry that woman. So it seems that this girl will be married to me."

This is the sort of purity one gets only if one follows pure feelings and expresses them in true words, and does exactly as one says. If one learnt this and kept this consistency, then one would grow; one would become more serious and acquire more strength of character. This brings unity into a man and creates a sort of depth, and to this unity and depth of the individual the glory of the Absolute descends, and then one manifests all around everything that one knows of the glories of the Absolute.

Does what you have said signify a certain order of action? You mentioned twice: "Beginning with feeling, and then speaking what you feel and doing what you say." Is this order important in this connection?

It is not only important but necessary, for this is the ultimate thing that happens—it belongs to the pattern of nature. This is how things do happen, but by ignorance we do not follow this sequence and make complications for ourselves. Ordinary man does not go by this sequence. Those who want to go on the way should follow this sequence.

THE ELEPHANT AND THE CROCODILE

In trying to dedicate one's actions to the Absolute, one finds there is much unworthiness in one's thoughts, words, and casual postures and actions that one could not possibly dedicate to the Supreme Self. If one wants to do what one says and say what one thinks, it seems to be a full-time job!

In dedicating to the Absolute or to the Self, the most important part is the heart, and that is very simple. If that is properly attained in its simplicity, all the rest should not bother one, because nothing else is very important. One can see from so many examples that this is so. Here is one:

There was a great elephant who was proud of his size and

strength, but when he went to bathe he was caught by a croco-
dile in mid-stream and dragged out of his depth into deep water.
He was helpless and couldn't do anything, but just when he was
about to be drowned he happened to catch with his trunk a lotus
flower floating on the river, and offering that flower to the Absolute, to his God, he begged Him to save his life. So pure was
his offering, that God came running barefoot from His throne.

One might wonder how one could dislodge the Absolute
and cause Him to come barefoot from His throne by just a little flower! But it was not the flower, it was the spirit behind the
flower, it was the heart which prayed.

There is another story of a saint called Rantideva, who took
just a little water, and offered this small amount of water and,
in doing so, achieved liberation—only a pot of water as against
full realization!

One can see the same thing in one's ordinary life. A father
does everything he can for his child, and while being fed seated
on his lap, the child might take a little of the food and try to put
it into his father's mouth. Now, that tiny piece of food which
the child puts into the father's mouth pleases him so much that
he goes into ecstasy; all the troubles brought on by the child are
forgotten.

LAKSHMAN'S CHILDHOOD

When Lakshman, the younger brother of Rama was a child he
had a bit of a temper and one day he got very cross. He picked
up a stick and broke all the chandeliers in the palace, and anything made of glass, and did a lot of damage. The minister re-

ported to the king, his father, that just now they had seen this bad boy, Lakshman, in hot temper doing all that damage. The king told them to call the priests to celebrate the occasion by opening the doors of the treasury, distributing alms and, he added, "Let's have music and singing."

The astonished minister said, "I hope I expressed clearly what Lakshman has been doing." He thought the king was trying to be funny! But the king said, "Well, it's nice to see that my small son is growing up and has gained enough strength to do all these things. So don't you think this is a cause for rejoicing, and that we should rejoice together?"

So we must understand that the Absolute is not really interested in the details of the bad behaviour of mankind during the growing-up period! The Absolute or the Universal Self wants the human heart in its simplicity and directness. When that has been dedicated, everything will follow in the course of time, and one need not worry whether man's actions are small or big, good or bad, efficient or inefficient. That doesn't matter—the real dedication He requires is only of the heart.

THE BOY WHO WROTE TO THE ABSOLUTE

Would it be a practical plan of action to offer every action to the Absolute, that is, to hold the memory of the Universal Self, as a husband holds the memory of his wife?

We would greatly benefit by doing what is meant by offering all actions to the Universal Self! This is like a son who hands over the whole amount he earns to his father; the father then decides what his son's needs are and fulfils them very gladly. It is the same with the Universal Self. Here is an instance from real life:

There was a boy who had lost both his parents. He was very poor and wanted to enter a school to study. To do this he needed money for school fees and stationery but he had no money to buy them. All this caused him considerable worry. By chance he met a mahatma and he expressed his difficulties to him. The mahatma gave him some advice. He told him to write a letter to the Absolute. "Write the letter like this: 'Oh, my Father, the Absolute, please help me, I am very poor, my parents are dead, I have no money to pay my school fees, buy books, or continue my studies.' "

"How shall I post it?" he asked.

"Address it to the Absolute," the mahatma told him.

He did as he was told, writing the letter and addressing it simply to the Absolute. He then put it in the post box. The box was cleared and the letter taken to the postman who sorted them. He said, "Where is this place that the Absolute lives?" They presented this to the postmaster who asked them to bring the boy to him. The boy was brought to the postmaster, who adopted him and looked after all his expenses. The boy had the highest education, eventually becoming a judge. The judge himself told me this story.

In the same way if we offer and dedicate all our actions to the Absolute then in that case He fulfils all our needs and the needs of those who are connected with us.

Offering all our actions to the Absolute doesn't mean that after earning some wages we give it all away as an offering to the Absolute. It is just that we mentally offer our wages to the Absolute. The money is yours and if we use it after offering it to the Absolute it would become something like a gift from the Absolute. We should adopt that attitude: having learnt that we should treat it as belonging to the Absolute, use it as a gift from Him, not as our own.

Take the joint family in India. The custom of joint families was universal in olden times but today this tradition is breaking up. The idea was that each member of the family gave over whatever he had and made it available to the family and the head of the family saw to his needs. In the case of someone who did not earn and could not deposit any money with the family, no one worried and he would still receive what he needed. The same applies to offering all of our actions to the Absolute. If we dedicate our actions to Him then our worldly requirements are taken care of by the Absolute.

15

Renunciation and Giving Up

PRAJAPATI AND HIS SON KACH

It is possible in the night to be still for quite a long time, but the feeling of 'I' remains there in the stillness.

When one knows that one is still one is not still, and when one knows that one is at peace, one has not reached it because the great barrier remains, this recognition of 'I' and its relation with peace and stillness. In complete peace or stillness there is no 'I'!

Prajapati was the teacher and priest of the gods. His son, Kach, having gone through the proper education in the Vedic and Upanishadic texts, and having acquired all the knowledge that was to be acquired, came back to his father. His father asked him what he intended to do. Kach said, "The essence of all I have learnt is that renunciation is the best medium for life, so I would like to go the way of renunciation." But he would not take up the activities of the priesthood, and he would not help in the household activities either; he just stayed in the house.

After some time, his father asked him whether he had really renounced everything. As far as the father could see, his son had renounced all work, but he still kept on living, eating, and using the amenities of the house. "So what about that?" The son said, "All right, I will renounce the house," so he left the house and went into the jungle and stayed there.

Then, after another interval, his father visited him there and asked him what the situation was. The boy said, "I can't say I have acquired complete peace, so it seems I have not yet renounced everything." The father said, "Yes, of course, it seems so—your renunciation is not complete, otherwise peace would descend on you." So Kach renounced the clothes which he wore, the food he ate, and all activity, yet he could not get real peace of mind.

"Now," he said, "the only thing left to renounce is my body, so I must renounce the body," and he prepared a funeral pyre intending to jump into it. His father suddenly appeared and asked him if he was sure that this would be the final renunciation. The son asked, "But once I have given up the body, what else will remain to bind me to worldly things?"

His father replied, "Your subtle body is not going to die with your physical body, and the activities of the subtle body (which has desires) will make it keep on wandering, and will not subside after the body is burnt. You will get another body when you are dead, because there will be some desire in your subtle body, so burning the body is not the final answer—you are not going to get rid of this existence."

So the son said, "Well, what should I do if I cannot achieve renunciation, what else should I do?"

The father then said, "At last you have asked me a question, so now it is possible for you to learn something! Give up all your learning, and the final giving up, the final renunciation, will be the giving up of the very idea of renunciation. *You* are not giving up anything, everything is given up. By the idea of renunciation you are holding something in preference to other things. In fact, you are not renouncing; you are holding on very tightly to something lesser."

His father told him that to give up everything, you have only to give up the feeling of giving up. Your ego, which is trying to give up everything else, is still with you. Once you give up ego, then there is nothing of yours to give up.

It seems to take a long, long time! Some people perhaps are more egoistic than others. What is it that gives up? What is it that surrenders?

That which is never absent from anywhere.

And part of that substance is in me?

Yes. A part of that substance is within you and also you are within it. It is like the water of the Ganges and Ganges water in a bottle. Break the bottle and there is no separate trace of that water when mixed in the Ganges. As long as we associate the Self with the body, senses, and mind, desire or the feeling of 'I,' ego, we are separated and bottled up. Give up ego and there is no separation.

The creation is such that everything is there in its own right, everything has a purpose and must fulfil its function; so it must keep on rotating, it must be used. Use everything, and give up the idea that you are renouncing. Don't hold on to anything in this creation; that can only be done by this final renunciation of giving up the idea that you own anything. In fact, you own nothing. Everything belongs to the Absolute, everything is permeated by the Absolute; you use whatever you need, and the rest simply belongs to Him. This we must keep in mind when we think of renunciation.

To get peace on the subtle and causal levels it is clearly necessary to give up. The Shankaracharya has said, "Giving up can be done emotionally and intellectually at all times and in all conditions. Practise giving up all the time, by regarding the body, the mind, and the heart as belonging to the Absolute and so offering all these back to him." Even a little of this is found to be more effective than anything else. How can we make ourselves do more of it?

This observation is in keeping with the spirit of the first Upanishad, the *Isha*. The first two verses of this carve out the central core of what can be said to be the essence of Indian philosophy. The complete *Bhagavad-Gita* which we know, is almost an explanation of these two verses from this Upanishad.

The same thing given in these two verses is also given in the *Bhagavad-Gita*. Here Krishna says, "Whosoever sees the world in me, and sees me in the world, he alone knows me, and he alone will transcend, and be relieved of the turmoil of this universe. He will be in bliss and he will have everlasting life."

The essence of the first two verses of the *Isha Upanishad* is that all this universe is filled with the Absolute. If one takes anything in the world and looks into its construction, one will ultimately reach the state where one will find the Absolute in everything.

For example: you can take cloth. Cloth is made of thread, thread is made of cotton, and the cotton-boll comes from the earth, and the earth is made of water, water comes from fire, fire from air, air from space, and this comes from manifest nature, which comes from the unmanifest, which is in the Absolute.

So, if you keep on looking into anything, you will ultimately come to the Absolute, that which prevails in everything. This is the process through which all things are manifested. In fact, the Absolute is not just within matter; it is everywhere. It is not only the efficient cause, but the material cause also. Both are the Absolute, so the Absolute is within and without and the Absolute is everything.

The *Isha Upanishad* says that the universe is permeated by the Absolute. Whatever one sees in creation, whatever moves— one should use it fully and enjoy this Absolute everywhere, but one should enjoy it with renunciation. One should not try to hold it or covet it. One need not try to possess it; enjoy it—and give it up. So giving up is the most simple philosophy which promises complete fulfilment of the individual's life, also liberation after having enjoyed it. This is the meaning of that first verse.

The next verse says that, if one could live like this by en-joying the Absolute and giving up, one would desire to live a hundred years and, having lived this way, none of the actions which the individual has to undergo during these hundred years would bind him at all. There is no bondage for, in fact, he is already liberated; he lives in liberation, and when the body is finished with, he goes forth with liberation. Indeed nothing will bind him, so this observation which you have given is the cent-ral philosophy. If one could practise it all day, all the time, one would experience liberation within, and the real liberation from the body at death.

It seems that the 'personal servant,' the moving mind, can be purified, and to some extent controlled, by attending to one's own small routine actions: how one sits in meditation, how one moves and walks and talks as well as what actions one permits. Even a little of this practice, combined with keep-

ing the Absolute, who witnesses everything, in the memory as often as poss-
ible gives most rewarding results which make one long for complete union
more than anything else. Would His Holiness say that I can get this union
by continuing the way I am going or is something more required? In other
words (like Prajapati's son Kach near the end of the story), I am at last
asking the question: "Well, if I cannot renounce this way, what else should
I do? Am I also holding on to something very tightly instead of renounc-
ing it?"

Giving up is nothing except understanding the real meaning of 'giving up.' Ordinarily if we give up a certain thing we immediately develop an attachment to something else.

Kach's giving up was originally a giving up of external
things, therefore he did not find peace even when he gave up
all of them. But when he understood the real significance of giving up, he found that by giving up the very 'I-ishness' (ego) of
giving up, the giving up of all the things connected with the ego
followed as a natural consequence. This is true giving up.

Subsequently, Kach's practical life was that of an ideal man,
namely carrying out all the duties and obligations of a practical
life without any feeling of 'I' in his mind.

At the start, when a man in training goes on duty for the first
time he finds difficulties, but with further practice he is able
to act naturally and appropriately as his experience ripens.
Ultimately he achieves mastery and purity in this art.

By continuing practice of this kind we are able to discover
our own powers. This is the advantage of 'giving up' in practical life.

KUNTI'S WISH

Recently I have come to see more and more that it is taking things person-
ally which is the main barrier to development. Trying to help others is now
more important in terms of time and interest, but so much of this is really
wasted by this personal approach. I feel it is the meditation which has led
me to see this, and the longing to be free grows more and more but how can
you leave the personal quickly when you see it? I feel the idea of 'The
Monkey in the Tree' and listening to the prompting within should answer
my question. I hope the Shankaracharya can expand on it.

It would be wrong to say that the personal approach in this
work makes it wasted, for nothing can go to waste. Whenever
one takes anything on a personal level, or works from a personal
approach, one creates a limitation based on the physical world
and this will narrow things. This limited world of limited service will create only a limited effect.

If one is fortunate enough to see this personal angle as a
limited field then one starts looking for a broader, more general approach, the subtle world, the world of knowledge and
vast potentiality. If one could cross over to the general world
from the personal world, one would find that the field of service and sphere of influence becomes extensive. Every human
being is very much like the Absolute. The existence of this
creation is the desire of the Absolute to manifest itself and
enjoy. The same is true of all individuals. Everyone in the universe desires to become manifest and be happy. It is only towards this that all our activities are really directed. There is no
exception.

In the *Mahabharata* we find a curious story of a different type, but even that ultimately proves the point:

The great war was over and the victorious Pandavas took charge of the state. Their mother Kunti was asked by Shri Krishna to pray for a boon. She prayed for suffering. Shri Krishna observed that she might be doing so due to emotional imbalance, so he asked her again to reconsider and pray for something reasonable. Kunti replied that she was being perfectly reasonable in asking for suffering because there was no greater joy than being in the company of Krishna. Now, due to the victory, all material wealth and honours would be readily available to her and she might soon become attached to them. In fact, these material pleasures are not conducive to real liberation. If she could be given suffering, she would remember Krishna more often and would be able to see him and get his advice which she was sure would lead to the greatest happiness of all. So in fact she was praying for suffering only to ensure ultimate happiness!

Thus one can see that ultimately everyone without exception wants to improve and be happy. Not many people can appreciate this point. If one just accepts suffering and trouble, in fact one is working for a deeper happiness, and if one tries to organise things only to enjoy worldly happiness, one is working for a more painful bondage and suffering. Dark night brings in the glorious morning and warm bright days turn into dark nights.

It seems better to start from the dark and end with glorious light! If one sees that the personal approach does not bring in enough light and happiness, one should change over to a more general view. There is a further step to progress to the abstract view or truly universal view in its manifestation and happiness.

ALESKO AND THE TURTLE

Poverty need not mean misery, because if devotion develops in it, the image of God begins to live in the soul, just as the image of an object lives in a mirror. And a man thus possessing the image of the Almighty in his heart could no longer be called poor. But a poor man who entertains desires is certainly miserable, while a poor man with no desires at all is happy.

In olden times, there lived in China a man called Alesko. He kept nothing with him except a piece of gunny (jute sacking) to wrap around his body. The king needed someone who had no personal ambitions to manage the affairs of his kingdom. When he heard about Alesko, he wanted to try him and sent his men to call him. They found him playing with turtles in a pool.

"Lucky man," they said, "your days of poverty are over. His Majesty, the King, has summoned you to appoint you as his prime minister."

Alesko said, "Is it true that His Majesty keeps a turtle wrapped in a sheet of gold, and worships it every day?" "Yes, it is true." "Is that turtle alive or dead?" "It is dead, of course." "Would any one of the turtles you see here like to be kept like that while it is alive?" "No." "If even an animal would not give up its natural surroundings for being kept in gold, how do you expect me to do so? That turtle is dead, as you say. Similarly, I can also surrender my liberty only when I am dead."

Accepting flattery in order to escape poverty is to kill one's own life.

Where the *Bhagavad-Gita* prescribes 'giving up,' it also explains how to give up. What we have to give up is the desire to derive benefit from our actions, not the actions themselves. If we were to give up actions but continue to indulge in desires, then we would simply be pretending to give up. Before undertaking an action, an ordinary worldly man always tries to assess what benefit is going to accrue to him as a result of that action. But a realized man undertakes it as a matter of duty, with no desire for its consequential benefits.

Before trying to do good to others, we should first try to improve ourselves. We cannot save a drowning man if we cannot swim ourselves.

Correct attitudes make for real wealth. One who possesses this wealth is never poor.

The King Who Gave Away His Kingdom

A king who had grown old decided to abdicate his throne and become a recluse. He proclaimed that he would give away his kingdom to the first man who came to see him at eleven o'clock on the morning of the seventh day. Many people were attracted by this offer and they set out with the intention of appearing before the king at the appointed hour.

But the king had laid out a well constructed plan to select the most suitable person. On the way to his palace, he had built a beautiful pool with lotuses blooming—so beautiful that people were tempted to stop there and have a dip in it. Then the way led through a market which contained the best possible garments, which anybody could take free. The third stop was a big dining hall with luscious foods and drinks laid out. The fourth was a big bedroom containing voluptuous furnishings and bedding. In the fifth there was beautiful music provided. The sixth contained gold and jewellery. At all these places, people stopped to help themselves, and lost time or forgot their quest.

But one man, who was the last to start, overcame all these temptations, went through all the gates and met the king at the appointed time. To him the king formally handed over his throne and went away to the forest. The first act of the new king was to put under arrest all the people who had started out to see his predecessor, on the charge that they had taken things which did not belong to them. Thus renunciation brought him a kingdom.

We want pleasure but we get pain instead. This is because each pleasure contains the seeds of pain. The seeds of a thorny plant do not show any thorns. The thorns appear only much later when the seed has germinated and has grown up into a tree.

Thinking over the story of that one man who went through the gates to get the keys of the kingdom from the king himself, I had understood that this 'one man' was the individual Self and the king was the Universal Self. Is this correct?

The gates are the covering layers of manifested nature, such as the five elements, earth, water, etc., and mind and intelligence, enclosing in the most inaccessible layer of the soul the individual Self and the Universal Self. The individual actually sits in the lap of the universal, but the trouble is that the individual, in spite of such close proximity, possesses an external outlook and worries about those external layers of manifested nature. If the individual could turn his eyes inwards through meditation, then he would see where he is, namely in the very lap of the Universal Self. Then the gates would cease to matter and there would be a state of unbroken joy all round.

In true love you always give and don't demand in return. By giving, you allow things to happen. Love of the Absolute makes the desire to enjoy the riches of creation unnecessary, for all that would have already been offered to the beloved, the Absolute. In this way greed and attachment would not arise. Those who learn to give up greed and attachment break their bondage and emancipate themselves, or realize themselves. True lovers never go to sleep while waiting for the beloved! One must learn this lesson well—that one never demands anything in return for one's love and then, only, does one get all one needs for a good and happy life.

So it's not true love, but demanding love which constitutes attachment. Love is good when free from attachment?

When people love someone, they forget that real love means no demands on the beloved.

THE KING'S EXHIBITION

The happy certainty and realization that "I have nothing of my own" seems to open all doors. This first feeling is surely the emotional individual aspect, and must it not be followed by the universal aspect, "The whole universe belongs to me"? This brings great joy.

There was a king who organised a great universal exhibition. He invited exhibits from all over the world, and stalls of beautiful things were arranged. People assembled there to buy whatever pleased them.

There was one particular man who used to move round the stalls and examine them intimately, and yet he bought nothing. He went round day after day. People wondered why this man kept on looking at things but never bought anything. They tried to persuade him, but he said he would only buy when something really satisfied him. He kept up his search, and when only two days remained some people reminded him he had very little time left; he had better make his choice quickly or he would lose the chance of buying anything at all. He said he wanted to wait to see what really suited him or pleased him. This went on till at the last moment, when the stalls were about to be closed forever, he went to the king who had organised it all, and he held the king's hand. He said, "This hand has organised such a beautiful exhibition, I want to buy it," and he asked the price.

The king said it was very difficult for him to imagine that he himself was on sale, or that his hand could be for sale. There were other things to be bought, not the king. But the man said, "It is you who have brought about such beauty so I want you, not the things." The king said, "If you really want me you can have me only for love, not for money." So the man accepted and he surrendered himself with great devotion to the king, and then because he surrendered himself he won the king and then all the things in the exhibition which belonged to the king also belonged to him; he had no reason to buy anything any more because everything was his own. He could use whatever he wanted whenever there was a need for a particular thing to be used. He did not have to buy, he did not have to claim, he did not have to collect. It is only by surrender to the Absolute through love that one wins everything—that is the way we need to go.

Everybody wants to know why this has to be at the last possible moment,
just before closing time?

Although it is usually seen that things are recognised at the
last moment this does not mean that the things were not there
all the time. In the beginning everybody knew this, and everybody was devoted, but in the course of history this devotion was
lost and now they have to search. It is very like ordinary things
in one's house. People have their things, but sometimes, somehow these get lost, and they have to keep searching until they
find them. Once they are rediscovered people start to enjoy
them, having found them, although in fact they were there all
the time, and never lost. Things are never lost—nothing is
lost—it is only ignorance or forgetfulness through which we
seem to have lost them. It is not always at the last moment that
things are remembered, but better late than never.

Once you win over the Absolute by love, only then do you
get everything, but people usually stop for little things and give
up the pursuit of love.

When a child is really hungry, he won't settle for anything
but his mother, no matter how attractive the toys may be. When
he cries for his mother, she has to run to feed him no matter how
busy she is with other things. Love is direct and there is no room
for rewards or demands.

16

Unity and Nondualism

THE ARROW MAKER AND
THE MARRIAGE PROCESSION

To meditate is to be, to be one, one without a second. Here is
an example:

In very ancient times when Dattatreya was walking along a
street a marriage procession came by. He stopped at the door of
a shop where arrows were being made. The owner was busy
doing his work and did not bother to look at the procession. After
it had passed, Dattatreya wanted to know why this man did not
enjoy the merry procession. He asked if he had seen the marriage procession? The shopkeeper said no. He also said that he
had not even heard any noise because he had been busy shaping the point of the arrow. In shaping the point he became one
with it, and the sensory world did not exist for him at that time.

The same applies to meditation. In meditation one is just
one. One becomes the Self. The method of meditation is only
a process by which this is made possible. The Absolute meditates and becomes the creation; we meditate and become the
Absolute.

VYASA'S SON

Shri Sukadeva was the son of the famous author of ancient times, Shri Vyasa. Shri Sukadeva was a child prodigy who had already attained Self-realization. So, as soon as he could, he started running off into the forest to become a recluse.

But he was the only child of Vyasa, born to him in his old age after waiting for an heir all his life. Seeing him thus running away, Vyasa was grief-stricken and ran after him crying, "My son! My son! Come back!"

But Sukadeva went on without looking back. A river lay in his path. Some women were bathing in it naked. They saw Sukadeva passing close to them, but they did not pay any heed to him and continued to enjoy their bath. Subsequently Vyasa also reached the river in his pursuit of Sukadeva. But on seeing him, the women hid themselves behind trees and hurriedly put on their clothes.

Vyasa asked them why they did not mind the presence of his young son when they were without clothes, and why clothes became necessary before an old man like him? The women replied that Vyasa's son saw only his own Self in them. Although Vyasa was old that part of him which responded to the difference between a man and woman still continued to affect his vision.

Thus if we see differences in worldly things—'this is this, that is that'—instead of seeing everything as part of our own Self, then there will be things which we like and things which we dislike. The conflict between these likes and dislikes leads to unhappiness.

THE RICH MAN AND THE MAHATMA

A person who practises devotion uses his speech only to express the properties of the Absolute, and his eyes only for seeing Him everywhere.

In this way he is practising devotion everywhere, whether he is in a forest or at home. You are listening to this talk about the Absolute. This is also worship. But no action by itself is worship. Fill every act with the spirit of devotion, and every act becomes an act of devotion. Thus growing crops in a field, sitting in a shop selling things, etc., and all such activities can be converted into worship if they are done with a spirit of service to the Absolute.

Devotion is a power of the heart. Let this single power drive all your actions, just as a single electric main drives all the machinery in a factory.

When we give up the world in quest of devotion, the giving up should be mental and not merely physical. Physical giving up, without a corresponding mental attitude and with the mind still harbouring desires, is hypocrisy. It does not contribute to happiness.

In the mind of a busy householder, the idea of worship and devotion is sometimes lost sight of in the midst of daily engagements. The way to reverse this is to read holy works like the *Bhagavad-Gita* or the Gospels. This should be done as a daily routine by anyone who wants to practise devotion.

A rich man used to go to a mahatma, but he talked to him only about his household affairs. The mahatma asked him the reason for this and he replied that it was because the people of his household loved him very much; therefore they were always uppermost in his mind. The mahatma went to the rich man's house one day and gave a sewing needle to his wife. He said to her, "Your husband seems to be planning to take all his things with him when he goes into the next world. Tell him to carry this needle too, if he can, for my sake. I shall need it there for sewing my torn garments." When she told her husband this, he understood the truth about worldly belongings.

So, you should try to hoard what you can take with you, i.e. devotion, and not what must be left here, i.e. worldly possessions. Transfer your allegiance and affection to the Absolute. This is devotion. Under its influence everything undergoes transformation. Poverty becomes riches, poison becomes nectar. There is pain and suffering in the world only as long as faith in the Absolute is not there.

THE MAN WHO POSED AS THE SON OF A PRINCE

This body is like a big town, the habitation of many. It contains a whole world of living creatures within it. They all possess life and desire to live. Some appear harmful and some useful. They are constantly being kept in a state of dynamic equilibrium, and this equilibrium keeps the body fit. Any disturbance of the equilibrium causes disease; then compensating forces of nature arise which tend to set it right. Similarly, when the balance in the creation is upset, then the forces of the Absolute come into play to restore it.

Nature is constantly striving for perfection, never attaining it. Man also is part of nature. One who is ill, tries to get well;

one who is weak, tries to become strong; one who is poor, tries to get rich and so on. Thus, in every situation there is dissatisfaction, and there are corresponding efforts to overcome it and to improve things.

But the more we try to improve, the worse everything seems to get. We say we have progressed, but we also say that the olden days were golden days. Similarly, today which seems full of causes for dissatisfaction, will become a golden day tomorrow. Gandhi considered taxation in his day to be excessive and launched an agitation against it, but now that taxation is considered very light compared with today's.

The reason is that increase of material facilities does not contribute to happiness, instead it is taking a rational attitude that promotes happiness. If our planning is good, then even fewer facilities will be enough to create happiness.

Our efforts, however, are directed more towards looking good externally and less towards being so internally. Trying to look good outside, but remaining bad inside, is deception. Such attempts can only result in harm.

Once a well-dressed young man came to me and posed as a son of the prince of Avagarh. He said that he was stranded at the railway station as he had lost all his luggage, and he wanted a loan, promising to return it by telegraphic money order as soon as he got home. He was told to make himself comfortable at the ashram first and have his meal, and that we would consider later what we could do about it. By chance an employee of Avagarh State also happened to be in the ashram at that time. I asked him if he knew the man, and he denied all knowledge of him. The impostor then disappeared on some pretext and never returned.

The world, on the whole, is like this. People put on a good appearance outside and harbour ulterior motives within.

Trying to be good to our fellow beings is the first thing to do. One who does not serve his fellow beings is far from serving God. God gives us a decent human body at the time of our birth. But, by the time it is taken back, we have polluted it by all sorts of unholy actions committed during our lifetime. In this connection the saint and poet Kabir has said: "Everyone was given a shawl (the human body) to cover himself with, but all made it dirty during use."

Kabir also used it, but he was so careful that he returned it neat and clean.

THE LION CUB AND THE SHEEP

I would like to ask how to improve the quality of my attention, by better concentration in meditation, as I feel this would be a way to increase my capacity of love for the Absolute.

Although individuals do feel a separate identity, in reality there is only one identity and that is the Absolute. In our soul, the inner body, and the subtle body, we have this individual being, and because of ignorance and other influences it seems to feel different from the Absolute, and that is why it wants to unite with the Absolute. For this unity of the individual and the universal it seems as if the effort is being made by the individual himself. The individual, if indeed he does anything at all, only removes the impediments which block his vision of unity with the Absolute. In fact, the movement is only from the Absolute's side. It is the Absolute who reaches out to the individual himself.

Love or devotion should be developed by removing the impediments and that, of course, is possible through meditation and the attention which one brings into one's life. This, in a way, removes the separate identity of the individual which is composed of his name, his form, and his so-called nature. All these things have got to be given up for the real unity or for the real love towards the Absolute. The effort is, of course, made by the individual, but he really makes little effort. The greater effort is made by the Absolute, just as a small person or a child has short legs, so he can take only small steps. A big man can walk quicker and cover more ground. The same applies to the individual, who is a very small being, and the Absolute who has no limit. This is how the unity of the individual and the Absolute should be made.

All individuals are the Absolute themselves, and so are you. It is only a question of realizing that one is the Absolute. To realize that, one has to do away with those impediments, and to illustrate this here is a story about a lion cub:

Once, in the forest, a lioness who had several cubs went off to search for food, and while she was away one of the cubs strayed and got into the middle of a flock of sheep. The cub followed the sheep, and the shepherd, seeing the cub with the sheep, kept him. The cub behaved like the sheep because of the company of the sheep. The shepherd thought that if he remained in this forest, then one day the lioness would roar, and the cub, hearing the roar, would remember it was a lion and would attack the sheep. So he took the flock with the cub to another forest where he believed there were no lions.

One day, a lion did roar in this other forest, and all the sheep ran away, and the cub also tried to run away. The lion, in lion language, asked the cub to stop, and said, "Why are you afraid of me? There is no need—you are not a sheep—you are a lion, like me. If you are not sure I can show you." So he took him to a pond and the little lion saw in the reflection that he had the same face and same characteristics as the one who roared. Then the lion asked him to roar with him, so he learnt how to roar, and the whole personality and individuality of this little lion was completely changed and he started roaring like a grown lion.

All our efforts in the world are learning the language of the world, which is like the language of the sheep and the life of sheep. By good company—the company of saints, and through the discourses—we learn to give up the language of the world and take to the language of the spirit. Once we have learnt, and have seen how saintly people who are much closer to the Absolute conduct their lives, we can also be like this young lion and start behaving like a proper lion, because we are all proper lions by nature.

RAMTIRTHA SHARING HIS SALARY

The perfection with which we make preparations for unity with the Absolute depends on the relationship we establish with him, so that there is a feeling of universal brotherhood. In everything, everywhere we see the Absolute. The feeling you have for your family grows to include your community, then your nation, and then the whole world: from being limited we become unlimited and the whole world becomes our family, and we have the feeling, "Everything is mine, and I belong to everybody."

For example, there is the story of Swami Ramtirtha. He was a teacher at a college and he believed in the practice of universal brotherhood. Whatever salary or pay he earned, he tried to help everyone with it. He used to put it on the table so that anyone who needed money could take it.

His wife said, "I have prior right, why do you not put the money in my hands?" But Swami Ramtirtha replied, "It is for everybody and you are one of everybody; if you need it, you can also take it. I see God in everybody so how can I keep anything back? It is not that I am trying to help others, but because I keep seeing God!"

So in this way we can spread what we acquire to cover the whole universe. The Absolute can reveal himself in various forms; universal brotherhood just because it is universal doesn't mean that everything becomes just the same in all cases. The Absolute takes different forms and to each form we have to adjust our attitude accordingly. If the Absolute comes in the form of a child, then we have to greet him with love; if he comes in the form of a servant, we see God in the servant but we should accept his service; if he comes as a learned man he needs respect and we have to adjust our behaviour accordingly. If we are in the world, whatever our role, fulfilling that role is service to the Absolute.

KRISHNA AND SUDAMA

Could His Holiness say more about Advaita, nondualism?

The philosophy of Advaita relates to the cosmos and our-selves. What we call Universal Self and individual Self are actually in substance one; in principle they are one but in practice they are two. In practice whatever we get we get from the cosmos because we are composed of the elements. That is the basic principle of the nondualistic Advaita philosophy.

Yes, it's very much a question of how to approach it. Reason tells me that I am not separate from the cosmos, but experience seems to show a difference. Is it a question of bringing the two views together?

That is true. By reason we know, but in practice we have to act as if there were two, otherwise it would be difficult to act in life. But whatever we may be doing we should remember we are one. That's the instruction.

The knowledge is there but while we are dealing in life we do not remember, we forget what we are, so it needs to be prac-tised. At present that knowledge remains knowledge only, but we can introduce it into our dealings by remembering that fact.

Lord Krishna had a friend, Sudama. It was a childhood friendship and once Sudama ate some food which was actually meant for both of them. He stealthily ate up Lord Krishna's share as well as his own. As a result of this there was great poverty and Sudama was deprived of worldly affluence. Then he was goaded by his wife to go and approach his old friend. He went, but he was so poverty-stricken and so weak that he didn't even have the strength to go the full distance, so he fell half-conscious on the way. Lord Krishna himself arranged for Sudama to be brought to him.

When Sudama arrived at the gates of Lord Krishna, the servants would not let him in, because Lord Krishna was living like a king and Sudama was a poor man dressed in rags. At every step he was stopped. Ultimately when he did get in and he met his friend Krishna, the two became one. They were very happy and Krishna worshipped his friend, honoured his friend. On seeing that their master honoured this visitor, the servants also started to revere the person whom they were obstructing a little while ago.

Now this parable is a story of the Universal Self and the individual Self. Because the individual is weak, he cannot get to the universal by his own efforts. He is dependent on the help of the universal. Wisdom is the wife in that story. The wife goads Sudama. Wisdom goads the individual to go to the universal. And when the individual returns to actual worldly affairs he finds everything arranged for him. Servants started arranging things for the visitor when they knew he was the old friend of the master.

17

Wisdom and Advice

THE MILLIONAIRESS WHO HAD DIABETES

When a doctor is dealing with serious or difficult diseases, he becomes very concerned with the result he is trying to achieve. How can we get over this dilemma?

The Self is, in fact, surrounded by three bodies, physical, subtle, and causal, and all the three bodies are interrelated. On the physical level there is a healthy state and a state of many diseases. On the subtle level of the mind, there are also diseases caused by wrong points of view as well as those resulting from physical diseases. In fact, ultimately, many physical diseases owe their origin to something wrong on the level of the mind. Physical illness must be treated by the appropriate physical means, mental illnesses by good ideas and improved attitudes and ways of thinking, and the causal body by firm emotions and emotional truths.

There are two kinds of patient, the one with a physical illness who takes the prescription or recommendation with a smile and in good faith, and there is the other kind of patient who does not accept the treatment and this attitude delays the process of healing. These people must be treated mentally as well as being given physical treatment.

There was a millionairess from Delhi who suffered from diabetes. She was very fond of sweets which she used to obtain secretly from her servants. This was unknown to her doctor and her family, who became very concerned, because the more her doctor treated her the worse she became, because she was secretly eating sweets.

A new doctor was called. He visited her before breakfast and examined her, and suspected that something was in her stomach though she denied having eaten anything. Her relatives also said she had had no food for three days. But in fact she had arisen early and obtained more sweets from the servants and eaten them.

The new doctor still suspected that she had something in her stomach. By persistent questioning of the servants, he found the true state of affairs and so was able to put the matter right.

As for the dilemma, there is none! If one attends to one's work, the result takes care of itself.

The Holy Man's Advice to the Cripple

A rich man had three sons, the youngest being a cripple. The father looked after the cripple well as long as he was alive, but after his death the cripple received no attention from his brothers and passed all his days lying on the doorstep crying for food and water. One day a holy man passed that way; the cripple told him his story and asked for advice. The holy man took him outside the village and made him sit under a banyan tree. He asked him to remain like that for three days without eating or speaking to anybody.

When people saw him sitting there motionless for three days, eating nothing and speaking to no one, they grew curious and thought that he must be a great mahatma. As the news spread, people from far and near came to have a look at him. So great were the offerings of fruit and sweets brought by them that a hundred men could live on them instead of one. The holy man gave him neither method nor teaching, but merely by doing what the holy man suggested the cripple's life changed for the better.

THE BRAHMIN WHO LEFT NINETEEN COWS

Mathematics and physics in the West have become so complicated that they bear little relation to the practical life of the householder. But recently we have met one or two professors of mathematics and physics who meditate with much benefit. It would be useful if we could prove to them that ancient wisdom could solve their problems more simply. You will, of course, know the following story with which we could perhaps begin, if our version is accurate.

There lived long ago, in the country of King Dharmasana, an old brahmin who had three sons and who possessed nothing in the world but nineteen cows. Before he died he called his sons and said, "My sons, I am in the mouth of death, so listen attentively. All I have to give you are these nineteen cows; divide them among you in this way: let the eldest take half of them, the next a quarter and the youngest a fifth share of them. But should there be any remainder left over, you must all three eat it; if not, all the cows are to be given to the king, and my curse will rest upon you." And saying this, that old brahmin died.

When after performing the rites of burial, they came together to divide the property, the eldest brother said, "Half of these cows, that is, nine cows and a half, are mine." The next brother said, "One quarter, that is, four cows and three-fourths of a cow, are mine," and the youngest said, "The remaining fifth, that is, three cows and four-fifths of a cow, are mine."

The eldest then remarked, "The sum of all these, added together, amounts only to eighteen cows and a fraction of a cow. But how is it possible for brahmins to eat the flesh of a cow, or how are we to take various pieces of a cow and leave it still alive? But unless we share in the correct proportion, all the cows must go to the king, and our father's curse will fall on us. Why did our father place us in so terrible a dilemma?"

After debating day and night, they at last put their problem to a holy man. After a moment's thought he replied, "Let the brothers borrow another cow. Then of the twenty cows, let the eldest take half or ten cows, the next a quarter or five cows, and the youngest a fifth or four cows. Then let them return the borrowed cow. Thus the nineteen cows will be divided according to the father's instructions, with no remainder. Each brother will receive more than by their own division, and finally the king will be pleased. For he is a just king and what would displease him more than that anywhere in his kingdom brahmins should kill and eat cows, let alone chop them up, and at the same time disregard their father's dying instructions?"

I used to think that this story was only a key to the laws of nature, for nature always prefers whole numbers to fractions. But lately I perceived another meaning also: that whenever we put any problem, however com-

plex, to the Absolute or to his representative, the holy man, the answer comes back in so new and simple a form that one gasps, "Why couldn't I have thought of that?"

Regarding the story of the brahmin and his sons, it has a psychological meaning also. The five organs of action, plus the five sense organs plus the five *pranas* (vital energies), together with mind, intelligence, memory, and ego make nineteen, and they constitute the body of the sons. These were the nineteen cows. The twentieth cow, which was borrowed and which facilitates the division, was wisdom and did not form part of the body. Naturally it was left out as it only facilitated the division and it did not actually enter it.

The mathematicians and the physicists should understand that in the laws of nature there are no oddities anywhere. There is, on the other hand, an evenness throughout. That is why natural laws are so amenable to reason and ultimately they all fit into one another so simply and beautifully. Ancient wisdom does help to solve problems easily. It is all contained in ancient *granthas* (books). But by simply reading them nobody can solve the problems, as the *granthas* contain *granthis* (knots) which can be undone only by experienced teachers.

For example, if arsenic is prescribed for the treatment of a particular disease, it takes a medical man to say in what form and in what dosage the arsenic is to be given.

These *granthis* or knots are sometimes introduced on purpose, illustrated in the next story of the buried gold.

THE BURIED GOLD

A rich man built a temple. On the Vijay Dashma day and at four o'clock in the evening, he buried four pots full of gold coins just where the shadow of the temple's pinnacle fell on the ground. He left a note in his will for his sons stating that he had buried four pots full of gold coins at four o'clock on the Vijay Dashma day at the pinnacle of the temple. They might take them out if and when they ran into financial difficulties.

Eventually the sons did run into financial difficulties. They broke the pinnacle and found nothing. Then they dug out the whole temple in search of the pots, still finding nothing. As they were in trouble for want of money, they talked to everyone about it. One day a mahatma passed that way and he also heard their problem. After inspecting the site carefully he asked them to rebuild the temple just as it was. This was easily done as all the materials of the old temple were lying there. Then he asked them to call him again on Vijay Dashma day, and they did so.

He saw where the shadow of the temple's pinnacle fell at four o'clock on that day, and asked the sons to dig there. The pots were found after digging down only a few feet.

All this shows that there are three kinds of good company. First is the physical which only hears and appreciates, the other is of knowledge which discriminates, and tries to put into practice, and the third is the truth or company of the Self which knows and practises and can show the way, for it holds the keys to all problems.

There are people who have some purity and light within and they naturally respond enough at least to appreciate the good words they hear. Due to lack of enough light they stop short and neither raise questions nor practise the teaching. This is the coarsest part of good company. The second kind raise questions because they think about keeping the teaching pure and making it more practical, and also they make efforts to practise the teaching.

True knowledge belongs to everyone and in fact everyone knows the truth, but in this phase of creation it has been forgotten. So the knowledge has always to be passed from one to another. Accordingly this tradition also has acquired it because it was passed down from the Creator and exists to this day. One has to inherit, be instructed, and then pass it on. Thus although it is always borrowed, yet it is in truth one's own. There is, of course, a danger in knowing that it is one's own knowledge, for one might become proud and claim it. This would make one incapable of appreciating further and finer knowledge.

The third kind of good company inherits in full and brings true knowledge into full practice (of creative thinking).

AJAMILA AND THE NAMING OF HIS SON

In Indian history the role of the holy men—the mahatmas—is very important. Mahatmas lead a special life, but they appear in ordinary life as well, and when this happens they always come with advice, some sort of helpful advice, so that without disturbing the life of the ordinary man or his frame of mind, they contribute something which is of direct use to the individual, even though he does not realize the importance of the advice given to him.

The story of Ajamila is an example of this helpful practical advice.

Ajamila was an ordinary man engaged in ordinary life, and not of any saintly disposition. Once a mahatma happened to come by his town and eat at his house and wanted, in return, to give him some helpful advice. So the mahatma asked him, "What is it that attracts you most? Is there anything to which you are attached, above all?"

Ajamila said, "I am most attached to my youngest son." So the mahatma asked him to call the youngest son by the name of Narayana. Whenever, therefore, he had to call this boy, he should call him by that name, and so he did.

There wasn't anything more that Ajamila was asked to do; he wasn't prescribed any discipline or other things, he was simply given this advice. At the time of his death, as usual, without knowing, he called Narayana, his little son, and because of this name, the messengers of Narayana (Vishnu) appeared and liberated him.

In India there are temples with carved stone statues of gods in them, and as part of their devotional practice people bow down before them and worship and pray. In fact, it is not the stone sculpture which is being worshipped, it is the idea of the god superimposed on this stone statue, and it is because of the devotion to this particular idea of god that they worship it. But as far as the names are concerned, the mantras, they are very potent even though there is no form attached to the mantra. In fact, the name Narayana stood for a mantra which, without realizing it, Ajamila used to recite in calling his son. Just as in meditation we are given certain words, the word has no form other than the vocal sound; it is not attached to any particular deity, or any particular meaning, it is only a sound, but it is a creative sound.

All sounds are creative, so when a mantra is given, this creative sound becomes the vehicle of transformation in the individual. Thus, because Ajamila used to pronounce the name Narayana, which is very like a mantra, the forces involved in the sound were made use of for his self-development. Just as with a fire—if you touch it, whether knowingly or unknowingly, it is bound to burn you, to hurt you. In exactly the same way, a mantra, whether you know anything about it or not, will come to your rescue if you utter it and lead you towards liberation.

THE MAHATMA WHO CRIED

When one is happy and has a warm glow, the physical limitations of the old flesh and old bones seem to be lessened by attending carefully to how one speaks, and how one moves. Is this how one can still serve the Self?

The Self is not bound by time, space, and change, so it never gets old, it never gets rusty; it is only the physical world which is governed by time and space and change. To be young or old is only relative to the body, but this does not really apply to the Self. When one is charged with emotional energy, or for that matter with intellectual energy, they bring about this glow of bliss with its warmth in the heart which spreads throughout the body. The body gets a little more attuned, and it works a little better than it can in ordinary circumstances, but the man who is charged with energy when the distraction is not there, is much more united with the Self, and the feeling of being old disappears and he works exactly in the same way that a young person would. This is the feeling of the Self—one behaves properly, one speaks properly, and this is the way not only to serve the Self but to be the Self.

There was a holy man, and one of his disciples lost a son. Full of grief and agony he went to the holy man and started crying. The holy man also started crying and weeping much more violently than the father himself. Having seen this, the father stopped crying and asked the holy man why he was crying. The holy man said he could not help it as he had the same feelings as the father for his son, as if his own son had died, so he too had this feeling—it was natural. The father stopped crying and went home feeling confident that he was not alone in his grief, others were with him, even the holy man.

Another man in the audience asked the holy man, after the father had left, why he had done such a thing, because a holy man should never show such outbursts of pleasure or pain, that is what he always advised everyone, and yet he had fallen into the same worldly habit.

The holy man said that if he had tried to give the father solace by wise words, it would not have gone really deep into the father's heart; he would have taken it in but his pain would have lasted longer. When the holy man started crying, the man found sympathy, and in sympathy the pain was shared and the weight of it made lighter, and then he did not feel alone in the world, so he need not worry and he would not worry. The holy man said the father's pain was real, but his was not, though he knew how to act in the drama very well, and it worked. His job as a holy man was very like that of a postman who delivers hundreds of letters, some of them bearing good news, some of them bad news, sad news, etc. Yet the holy man would never become involved though his face might change slightly when he delivered the letter, but he never got involved. One has to play the part, whatever seems most suitable at the time, but in reality the holy man is not involved with pain or pleasure in itself.

The same applies to a person charged with emotion; he will see that he acts like the Self, he speaks like the Self, or, one might say, he serves the Self.

THE MAN WITH THE LANTERN

Each person is provided with certain assets or talents to make use of for himself, his family, his society, his nation and so on. We all have to understand how much energy is available to us to use in a particular situation.

The principle is that one does not have to think about what one cannot do; one should always keep in mind what one can do.

There was a man who had to travel ten miles to attend to some urgent work. It was late at night and very dark. He took his lantern and went out of the house. He realized that it would be pitch dark for the whole ten miles to his destination. He thought of his small lantern and wondered how he could find his way in such darkness. Fortunately, a holy man passed by and enquired why the man was hesitating. The man expressed his fear of travelling ten miles with a lantern which shone only ten feet. The holy man pointed out that with each step the light would also move forward—it would always be ten feet ahead of him so he should not worry but just proceed. This he did, and reached his destination safely.

Whatever power has been given to the individual should be used in the best possible way. Electricity is provided through proper wires and connections, but if anyone tries to use a 110-

volt appliance to deliver 240 volts it will fuse. This means that individuals, having been given certain limits with which to manifest the glory of the Absolute, cannot claim or exert any extra power because they are not designed to do so. This each of us has to realize.

The ant has a particular measure of power and has to perform its activities within those limits. The elephant has been given a different measure and, accordingly, a different body. The ant cannot perform the deeds of the elephant, nor can the elephant perform the deeds of the ant.